1 Hello!

T0345704

A Foundation exercises

Vocabulary: The alphabet

1 Write the next letter.

z j *c* x r l o f u

1 a	b	*c*
2 d	e	
3 g	h	
4 j	k	
5 m	n	
6 p	q	
7 s	t	
8 v	w	
9 y		

2 Complete the names.

A	b	i	j	P	s

1 Ro _b_ bie   **4** L......ly
2 ......lex   **5** Ra......
3 A...ha   **6** Mrs ......atel

3 Follow the alphabet round. What name does it end on? Complete the sentence with the name.

Asha							Robbie	
z	y	x	t	o	p	q	h	k	z
d	e	f	c	n	a	r	l	m	y
c	l	g	r	m	b	s	k	f	x
a	b	s	h	q	l	o	t	u	v	w
i	o	i	j	k	f	m	g	n	e
q	r	u	v	x	j	s	x	w	y
z	y	w	g	i	h	p	d	t	z
Raj							Lily	

Hi. I'm ....

Grammar: The verb *to be*

4 Complete the sentences.

Hello. I'm I'm Alex. Raj
Robbie ~~What's~~

1

Hello. *What's* your name?

2 Hi. I'm ....

3 Hello. I'm ....

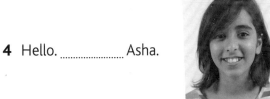

4 Hello. .... Asha.

5 .... I'm Lily.

6 Hi. ....

A Activation exercises

Vocabulary: The alphabet

1 Write the missing letters in each group.

1 **a** ..b.. **c** **d**

2 **e** .... **g** **h**

3 .... **j** .... **l**

4 **m** **n** **o** ....

5 .... **r** .... **t** **u**

6 ..... **w** **x** ..... **z**

English today

2 Complete the words.

| d | é | i | K | l̸ | o | y |

1 H e l l o.
2 H.......
3 O.......
4 B.......e.
5 G.......o.......bye.

3 Match the pictures with the words.

a

b

1 Goodbye. ....
2 Hello! ....

Grammar: The verb *to be*

4 Read and choose.

1 What ⓢ/ 'm your name?
2 My name 'm / 's Asha.
3 Hi, I 'm / 's Lily.
4 Your name 's / 'm Alex.
5 Hello, I *are* / 'm Raj.
6 I 's / 'm Robbie.

5 Complete the dialogues.

| Hello | I'm | ~~Lily~~ | Robbie | What's | your |

1

Hello, I'm ¹ _____Lily_____.
What's ² _____ name?

³ _____ Raj.

2

⁴ _____, I'm Asha.
⁵ _____ your name?

Hi, I'm ⁶ _____.

6 **Find and write the sentences.**

A: *Hello, my* _____ . *W* _____ ?
B: *I* _____ .

7 **Write the words in the correct order.**

1 Alex. I'm Hello,

Hello, I'm Alex. _____

3 name? your What's

_____

5 goodbye OK, Raj!

_____

2 Alex. Hi,

_____

4 My Raj. name's

_____

6 Alex! Bye,

_____

A Extension exercises

Vocabulary: The alphabet

1 Find and write the six missing letters of the alphabet.

C r V D

B i X F

j A K o

w s n Z

G p Q U

The missing letters:

1 ......
2 ......
3 ......
4 ......
5 ......
6 ......

2 Complete the sentences with the missing letters from Exercise 1. Then answer the question.

Hel___o. W___a___'s ___our na___e?

Your answer: _I_____

3 Write the names in alphabetical order.

| Raj | Lily | Miley | ~~Asha~~ | Robbie | Justin |

1 _Asha_
2 ....
3 ....
4 ....
5 ....
6 ....

Grammar: The verb *to be*

4 Write the dialogue in the correct order.

a Zac Efron? Hi, Zac!
b ~~Hello, I'm Pete.~~
c My name's Zac Efron.
d What's your name?
e Hi, Pete.

Pete: ¹ _Hello, I'm Pete._
Zac: ² ....
Pete: ³ ....
Zac: ⁴ ....
Pete: ⁵ ....

About you

5 Introduce yourself to a famous person. Write a dialogue. Find a picture.

You: ....
Famous person: ....
You: ....
Famous person: ....
You: ....
Famous person: ....

Vocabulary: Family members

1 **Write the words in the correct columns.**

| aunt | brother | father | grandfather | grandmother | mother | sister | uncle |

brother	*aunt*
....	....
....	....
....	....

2 **You are Alex. Write the names of the family members.**

Jerry   Janice

Eric   Sally   Peter   Patricia

Lily   Robbie   ALEX   Jake

1 brother	*Robbie*	**4** mother	....	**7** aunt	....
2 sister	....	**5** grandfather	....	**8** uncle	....
3 father	....	**6** grandmother	....	**9** cousin	....

3 **Choose the correct words.**

1 A: Who's (he)/ she?   **B:** My brother.

2 A: Who's he / she?   **B:** My aunt.

3 *He's / She's* my father.

4 A: What's his name?   **B:** *His / Her* name's Eric.

5 *He's / She's* my sister.

6 A: Who's he / she?   **B:** My grandfather.

B Activation exercises

Vocabulary: Family members

1 Write the letters in the correct order to make the family members.

1 nluec _____uncle_____
2 brerhot ....
3 rhoemt ....
4 isesrt ....
5 ocunsi ....
6 tuan ....

2 Find the correct stickers. Then complete the names.

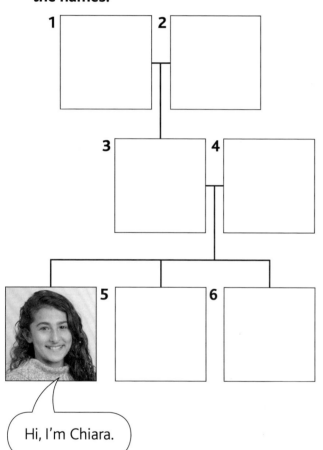

Hi, I'm Chiara.

1 He's my grandfather. His name's
P ....

2 Who's she? She's my sister. Her name's
E ....

3 Who's he? He's my father, E ....

4 Who's she? She's my grandmother,
P ....

5 He's my brother. His name's
A ....

6 She's my mother. Her name's
B ....

Grammar: The verb to be

3 Complete the sentences with *he* or *she*.

1 A: Who's ..._he_..?
   B: My father.
2 A: Who's ....?
   B: My sister.
3 ....'s my brother.
4 ....'s my grandmother.
5 A: Who's ....?
   B: My aunt.
6 ....'s my uncle.

4 Choose the correct words.

1 (His)/ Her name's Jerry.
2 His / Her name's Sally.
3 His / Her name's Raj.
4 His / Her name's Peter.
5 His / Her name's Asha.
6 His / Her name's Alex.

5 🔊 2/48 Listen and number the sentences.

She's my mother. ....
His name's Eric. ....
She's my sister. ....
He's my brother. ....
He's my dad. ...1...
Her name's Lily. ....
His name's Robbie. ...8...
Her name's Sally. ....

6 Put the dialogues in order.

1 What's his name? ....
   He's my grandfather. ....
   Who's he? ...1...
   His name's Jerry. ....

2 What's her name? ....
   Her name's Asha. ....
   She's my sister. ....
   Who's she? ...1...

7 **Look at the Beckham family tree and complete the sentences for Brooklyn Beckham.**

THE BECKHAM FAMILY

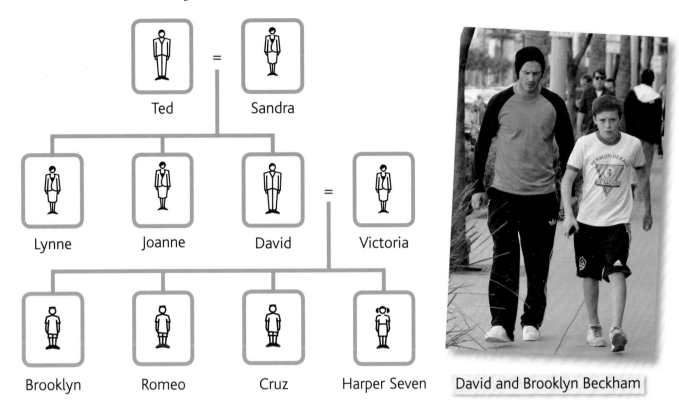

David and Brooklyn Beckham

1 David _'s my father_____.
2 Romeo _____.
3 Sandra _____.
4 Joanne _____.
5 Victoria _____.
6 Harper Seven _____.

8 **Write questions and answers for Brooklyn Beckham.**

1 (Romeo)   Question: _Who's Romeo_____?
             Brooklyn: _He's my brother_____.

2 (Lynne)   Question: _____?
             Brooklyn: _____.

3 (Victoria)   Question: _____?
             Brooklyn: _____.

4 (Ted)   Question: _____?
             Brooklyn: _____.

5 (Harper Seven) Question: _____?
             Brooklyn: _____.

6 (Cruz)   Question: _____?
             Brooklyn: _____.

B Extension exercises

Vocabulary: Family members

1 Make six family members. Use some letters more than once.

MO GR FA ER AND
BR SIS OTH TH TER

1 *MO + TH + ER = MOTHER*
2 ....
3 ....
4 ....
5 ....
6 ....

Grammar: The verb *to be*

2 Read and write the names.

The Name Game

That's my brother. What's his name? Write his name in box 1.

1 ....

That's my sister. What's her name? Write her name in box 2.

2 ....

That's my dad. What's his name? Write his name in box 3.

3 ....

That's my grandma. What's her name? Write her name in box 4.

4 ....

Hello! What's your name? Write your name in box 5.

? 5 ....

3 Complete the dialogues about Sam's family.

1 **Sam:** Who's [1] *he*?
  Mum: That's John. He's my brother.
  Sam: He's my uncle!

2 **Sam:** Who's [2] ....?
  Mum: That's Susan. She's my mother.
  Sam: [3] ....!

3 **Sam:** Who's [4] ....?
  Mum: That's George. He's my father.
  Sam: [5] ....!

4 **Sam:** Who's [6] ....?
  Mum: That's Jane. She's my sister.
  Sam: [7] ....!

About you

4 Draw pictures of your family members. Write sentences.

1

Her name's ....
She's my ....

2

....
....

3

....
....

8

Vocabulary: Days of the week; Numbers 0–50

1 Find and write the days of the week.

1  2  3  4

5 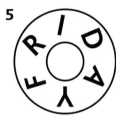 6  7

1 ....*Monday*.... 2 .... 3 .... 4 ....

5 .... 6 .... 7 ....

2 Write the numbers.

1
twelve
12

2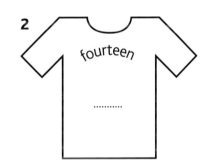
fourteen
....

3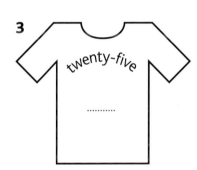
twenty-five
....

4
thirty-six
....

5
forty-one
....

6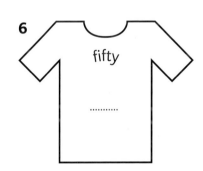
fifty
....

Grammar: The verb *to be*

3 Match the sentence halves.

1 How old are   a birthday today.
2 What day   b you?
3 It's my   c she?
4 You   d 're twelve.
5 She   e is it today?
6 How old is   f 's eleven.

C Activation exercises

Vocabulary: Days of the week; Numbers 0–50

1 Find and write the days of the week. Then write the missing day.

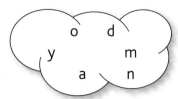 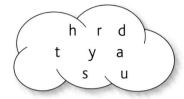 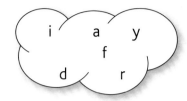

1 _Monday_

2 ....

3 ....

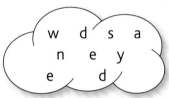 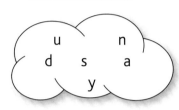

4 ....

5 ....

6 ....

The missing day: **7** ....

2 Write the days of the week in the correct order.

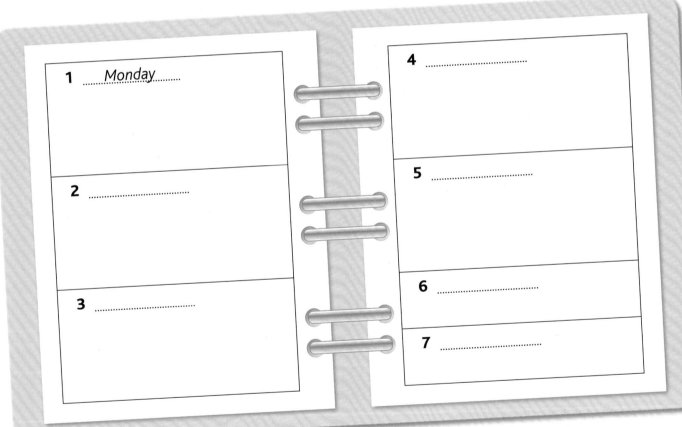

1 _Monday_

2 ....

3 ....

4 ....

5 ....

6 ....

7 ....

3 Write the words for the numbers.

1 15 _fifteen_

2 33 ....

3 18 ....

4 9 ....

5 47 ....

6 21 ....

Grammar: The verb *to be*

4 **Write the words in the correct order.**

1 old | am | How | I?

  How old am I?

2 is | What | it | today? | day

  ....

3 she? | old | is | How

  ....

4 is | birthday | My | on | Friday.

  ....

5 old | you? | are | How

  ....

6 my | It's | today. | birthday

  ....

5 **Complete the questions. Use *am, are, 's* or *is*.**

1 What _'s_ .... her name?
2 How old .... you?
3 What day .... it today?
4 How old .... she?
5 Who .... he?
6 How old .... I?

6 **Answer the questions about you and your family.**

You

1 What's your name?

  My name's ....

2 How old are you?

  I'm ....

Your ....

3 What's her name?

  ....

4 How old is she?

  ....

Your ....

5 What's his name?

  ....

6 How old is he?

  ....

7 **Complete the questions about Bella.**

SATURDAY
Bella – birthday
Twelve today!

Bella

What's [1] *her name* ....? Her name's Bella.

What day [2] ....? It's Saturday. It's her birthday today.

How [3] ....? She's twelve.

Complete the questions and answers.

FRIDAY
Luke – birthday
Eleven today!

Luke

What's [4] ....? [5] ....

What day [6] ....? [7] ....

....

How [8] ....? [9] ....

English today

8 **Complete the dialogues.**

| ~~birthday~~ Cool! no Really? Wow! |

Tuesday

Cassie: Hello, Simon. Happy [1] *birthday* ...!
Simon: What?
Cassie: It's your birthday today.
Simon: No, it's my birthday on Thursday.
Cassie: [2] .... Oh [3] ....!

Thursday

Cassie: Happy birthday, Simon!
Simon: [4] .... It's a big present, Cassie!
Cassie: How old are you today, Simon?
Simon: Twelve. How old are you?
Cassie: I'm twelve, too!
Simon: [5] ....

C Extension exercises

Vocabulary: Days of the week; Numbers 0–50

1 Write the numbers.

1

8	+	5	=	13
eight	and	*five*	is	*thirteen*

2

38	+	12	=	50
.....	and	.....	is	.....

3

17	+	27	=	44
.....	and	.....	is	.....

4

9	+	29	=	38
.....	and	.....	is	.....

5

14	+	11	=	25
.....	and	.....	is	.....

6

15	+	18	=	33
.....	and	.....	is	.....

Grammar: The verb *to be*

2 Write sentences.

1 How old / your aunt?
How old is your aunt?

2 She / thirty.
....

3 What day / it on Friday?
....

4 It / my birthday!
....

5 How old / you?
....

6 I / thirteen.
....

About you

3 Answer the questions about Kristen.

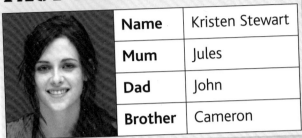

FACT FILE

Name	Kristen Stewart
Mum	Jules
Dad	John
Brother	Cameron

1 What's her name?
Her *name's Kristen Stewart* .

2 What's her mum's name?
Her ....

3 What's her dad's name?
His ....

4 What's her brother's name?
His ....

4 Complete the fact file for a friend or family member. Then write questions and answers.

FACT FILE

Name	
Age	
Mum	
Dad	
Sister	

1 What's *your name* ?
My name's ....

2 How .... ?
....

3 What's .... mum's .... ?
....

4 What's .... dad's .... ?
....

5 What's .... sister's .... ?
....

1 Read and answer *True* (✓) or *False* (✗).

Happy Birthday Jasmeen

Hello! My name's Jasmeen.
It's Friday today … it's my birthday!
I'm eleven.

My family
1: He's my dad. His name's James. He's thirty-six.
2: She's my mum. Her name's Elizabeth. She's thirty-four. She's nice.
3: He's my brother. His name's Michael. He's ten. He's cool!
4: She's my sister. Her name's Katrina. She's eight.

Jasmeen

1 Jasmeen is eleven.	✓	
2 Today is her birthday.	☐	
3 Her mum's Katrina.	☐	
4 Her dad's thirty-four.	☐	
5 Michael is her brother.	☐	
6 Her sister is eight.	☐	

Score: ...... /5

2 Write questions for Jasmeen. Use the question words.

1 My name's Jasmeen.   (What)   *What's your name?*
2 I'm eleven.   (How)   ....
3 He's my dad.   (Who)   ....
4 She's my mum.   (Who)   ....
5 He's ten.   (How)   ....
6 It's Friday today.   (What)   ....

Score: ...... /5

Colour one ring on Lenny's tail for each correct answer.

My score is ....!

2 Favourite things

A Foundation exercises

Vocabulary: Possessions (1); Colours

1 Look and write the words.

| ~~apple~~ TV football ice cream skateboard book |

| 1 _apple_ | 2 _____ | 3 _____ | 4 _____ | 5 _____ | 6 _____ |

2 Complete the words.

1 sk_a_teb_o_a_r_d
2 c___m___ut___r
3 b___ke
4 c___m___ra
5 f___ot___a___l
6 u___br___l___a

3 Read and colour the picture in Exercise 1.

1 (apple) It's green.
2 (football) It's orange.
3 (ice cream) It's yellow.
4 (book) It's pink.
5 (skateboard) It's purple.
6 (TV) It's black.
7 (clown) He's red, brown, white, blue and grey.

Grammar: *It's a / an*

4 Choose the correct words.

1 **A:** What's that?
  B: It's *a /* (an) apple.

2 **A:** What's that?
  B: It's *a / an* football.

3 **A:** What's that?
  B: It's *a / an* book.

4 **A:** What's that?
  B: It's *a / an* ice cream.

5 **A:** What's that?
  B: It's *a / an* skateboard.

6 **A:** What's that?
  B: It's *a / an* umbrella.

A Activation exercises

Vocabulary: Possessions (1); Colours

1 **Match the letters to make six possessions.**

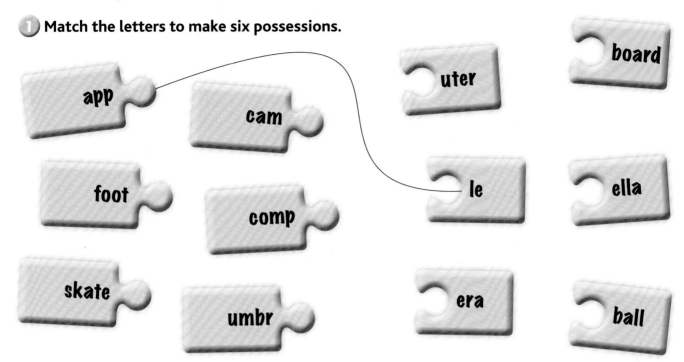

2 **Find and write the words.**

1 otllfoba   *football*

2 keib   ....

3 rbmlaule   ....

4 cie amcre   ....

5 atoaskebrd   ....

6 obko   ....

3 **Find the colours and write.**

..... *blue* .....

b l u e w h i t e
....
....
....
....
....
....
....
....
....

4 **Find the correct stickers.**

1 computer   2 apple

 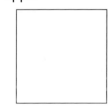

It's a _white computer_ . It's a ....

3 TV   4 skateboard

It's a .... It's a ....

5 umbrella   6 book

It's a .... It's a ....

Grammar: *It's a / an*

5 **Complete the sentences with *a* or *an*.**

1 It's _a_ computer.
2 It's ..... apple.
3 It's ..... TV.
4 It's ..... camera.
5 It's ..... umbrella.
6 It's ..... bike.

6 **Write the words in the correct order.**

1 green. | It's
   It's green. ....

2 that? | What's
   ....

3 a | skateboard. | blue | It's
   ....

4 red | a | It's | camera.
   ....

5 it? | colour | What | is
   ....

6 ice cream. | an | It's
   ....

English today

7 **Complete the dialogue.**

| know | right | done | ~~birthday~~ |

Robbie: Happy ¹ _birthday_ , Alex!
Alex: What's that? A present?
Robbie: Yes, that's ² ....!
Alex: I ³ ...., it's a skateboard!
Robbie: Well ⁴ ....!
Alex: What colour is it? It's purple! Cool!

8 **Write the answers.**

1 What's that? _It's a camera._

2 What's that? ....

3 What's that? ....

4 What's that? ....

5 What's that? ....

6 What's that? ....

A Extension exercises

Vocabulary: Possessions (1); Colours

1 Look and follow the lines. Write the possessions and their colours.

| 1 | 2 | 3 | 4 |
| 5 | 6 | 7 | 8 | 9 |

A acblk + egyr

B der + energ

C rpelpu + knpi

D cbalk + itwhe

E anroge + uble

F egyr + lebu

G owrnb + nkip

H dre + woylle

I ngeer + ngraoe

1	_TV_	_black and grey_	4	....	....
2	....	....	5	....	....
3	....	....	6	....	....

7	....	....
8	....	....
9	....	....

Grammar: *It's a / an*

2 Look at the answers to Exercise 1 and write mini-dialogues in your notebook.

1 A: *What's that?*
  B: *It's a TV.*
  A: *What colour is it?*
  B: *It's black and grey.*

About you

3 Tick (✓) your possessions at home. Then write about them.

computer	☐	umbrella	☐
football	☐	bike	☐
camera	☐	skateboard	☐

My computer is grey.

....
....
....

B Foundation exercises

Vocabulary: Everyday objects

1 Find and write the words.

rulerbagpenjacket
erasernotebook

1 _ruler_
2 ....
3 ....
4 ....
5 ....
6 ....

2 Find and write the everyday objects.

1 **peilnc seca**

...._pencil case_....

2 **lerru**

....

3 **emolbi pneho**

....

4 **daitcriony**

....

5 **noboteok**

....

6 **cmico**

....

Grammar: *Is it a / an ...?*

3 Complete the questions.

1 Is _it_ a pencil case?
2 ..... it a notebook?
3 Is it ..... eraser?
4 Is ..... a dictionary?
5 Is it ..... ruler?
6 ..... it a bag?

4 Complete the answers.

1   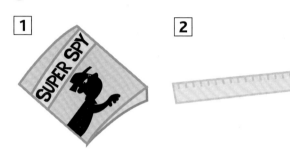

3   4   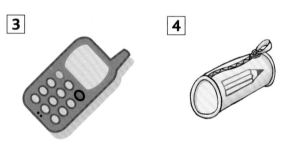

5   6   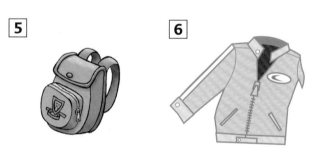

1 **A:** Is it a pen?
   B: No, _it isn't_ .
2 **A:** Is it a notebook?
   B: No, ...
3 **A:** Is it a mobile phone?
   B: Yes, ...
4 **A:** Is it a pencil case?
   B: Yes, ...
5 **A:** Is it a comic?
   B: No, ...
6 **A:** Is it a jacket?
   B: Yes, ...

Vocabulary: Everyday objects

1 Complete the crossword.

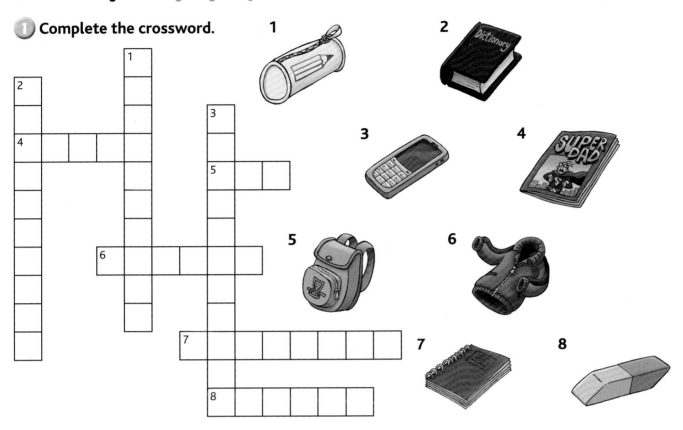

Grammar: *Is it a / an ...?*

2 🔊 2 49 Listen and tick (✓) or write the correct answer.

1 ~~comic~~ *notebook* ☐

2 eraser ☐

3 pencil case ☐

4 pen ☐

5 jacket ☐

6 dictionary ☐

3 Write the words in the correct order.

1 it | a | Is | book? | it | is. | Yes,
Is it a book?   *Yes, it is.*

2 No, | camera? | it | a | Is | isn't. | it
....

3 it | Yes, | umbrella? | Is | an | is. | it
....

4 a | notebook? | Is | it | No, | isn't. | it
....

5 an | Is | it | apple? | it | Yes, | is.
....

6 Is | computer? | it | a | it | isn't. | No,
....

4 Write questions and answers for Raj and Asha.

Raj: Wow! What's that? A present!
(book) [1] *Is it a book?*

Asha: (✗) [2] *No, it isn't.*

Raj: (camera) [3] ....

Asha: (✗) [4] ....

Raj: (mobile phone) [5] ....

....

Asha: (✓) [6] ....!

Raj: Cool!

Raj: Here's a present for you.

Asha: Cool! *(bag)* [7] *Is it a bag?*

Raj: (✗) [8] ....

Asha: (computer) [9] ....

Raj: (✗) [10] ....

Asha: (TV) [11] ....

Raj: (✓) [12] ....

Asha: Great!

5 Play the game with Robbie and Lily. Write their dialogues.

1 Robbie: Here's my word. Letter number one is 'p'.

Lily: (pen) [1] *Is it 'pen'?*

Robbie: No, [2] *it isn't.*

Lily: (purple) [3] *Is it 'purple'?*

Robbie: [4] ....

Lily: (phone) [5] *Is it 'phone'?*

Robbie: Yes, [6] *it is*!

2 Lily: Here's my word. Letter number one is 'b'.

Robbie: (bike) [7] ....

Lily: No, [8] ....

Robbie: (book) [9] ....

Lily: [10] ....

Robbie: (black) [11] ....

Lily: Yes, [12] ....!

3 Robbie: Here's my word. Letter number one is 'c'.

Lily: (computer) [13] ....

Robbie: [14] ....

Lily: (camera) [15] ....

Robbie: [16] ....

Lily: (comic) [17] ....

Robbie: [18] ....

English today

6 Complete the dialogue.

go	know	late	ready	Here's	up

Sara: David, let's [1] ......*go*......!

David: Sorry, Sara.

Sara: Hurry [2] ...., it's [3] ....!

David: I [4] .... Oh no!

Sara: What?

David: My jacket!

Sara: [5] .... your jacket.

David: Great! Thanks. I'm [6] .... now.

B Extension exercises

Vocabulary: Everyday objects

1 Look and answer the questions.

	A	B
1	SUPER DAD	(pen)
2	(eraser)	(jacket)
3	(pencil case)	(notebook)

1 What's B1? *It's a pen.*
2 What's A1? ....
3 What's B3? ....
4 What's A3? ....
5 What's A2? ....
6 What's B2? ....

Grammar: *Is it a / an ...?*

**2 Look at the pictures in Exercise 1.
Write questions and answers.**

1 notebook? (B1)
   A: *Is it a notebook?* B: *No, it isn't.*
2 comic? (A1)
   A: .... B: ....
3 pen? (B3)
   A: .... B: ....
4 jacket? (A3)
   A: .... B: ....
5 eraser? (A2)
   A: .... B: ....
6 jacket? (B2)
   A: .... B: ....

About you

3 Read the text and answer the questions.

My school bag

My school bag is great. It's blue and
white. It isn't big.
What's in my bag?
1 a dictionary
2 a pencil case
3 a pen
4 a ruler
5 a notebook

1 What colour is the bag?
   It's blue and white.
2 Is it a big bag?
   ....
3 What's number one?
   ....
4 Is number three a ruler?
   ....
5 What's number five?
   ....
6 Is number two a pencil case?
   ....

4 Write about your school bag.
1 What colour is your bag?
   ....
2 Is it a big bag?
   ....
3 What's in your bag?
   1 ....
   2 ....
   3 ....
   4 ....
   5 ....

Communication

Speaking: Greetings and personal information

1 Complete the dialogue.

Jake: [1] *Good afternoon.* I'm here for the Book club.

Teacher: Good afternoon. [2] ....

Jake: It's Jake Samuel.

Teacher: [3] ....

Jake: S–A–M–U–E–L.

Teacher: OK. [4] ....

Jake: It's 15890 645731.

Teacher: 15890 645731. OK. [5] ....

Jake: 27 Green Road.

Teacher: 28 Green Road.

Jake: No, it's 27. It isn't 28.

Teacher: Oh, sorry! 27 Green Road.

Jake: That's right!

~~Good afternoon.~~

How do you spell 'Samuel'?

What's your address?

What's your name?

What's your phone number, Jake?

Your turn

2 Complete the dialogue for you and your teacher.

You: Good [1] *morning.* I'm here for the English club.

Teacher: Good morning. (name?) [2] *What's your name?*

You: [3] ....

Teacher: (spell?) [4] ....
....

You: [5] ....

Teacher: (address?) [6] ....
....

You: [7] ....

Teacher: (phone number?) [8] ....
....

You: [9] ....

Teacher: Thanks!

Writing: Complete a form

3 Complete the form. Use the dialogue in Exercise 1 to help you.

Book club

Name: ....
Address: ....
Phone number: ....

4 Write and complete the form for you.

English club

Name: ....
....
.... : ....
....
.... : ....
....

1 Read and answer *True* (✓) or *False* (✗).

James: Sophie, here's a present. What is it?
Sophie: It's big. Is it a bag?
James: No, it isn't.
Sophie: Is it an umbrella?
James: No, it isn't.
Sophie: Is it a book?
James: No, it isn't!
Sophie: Er ... I know! It's a skateboard!
James: That's right! Well done!
Sophie: What colour is it?
James: Look!
Sophie: OK. It's pink and purple. Cool!

1 It's a big present.	✓	
2 It's a bag.	☐	
3 It's an umbrella.	☐	
4 It's a book.	☐	
5 It's a skateboard.	☐	
6 It's pink and purple.	☐	

Score: ...... /5

2 Which word is different? Choose.

Number one is 'computer' (black, pink and blue are colours).

1	black	pink	blue	(computer)
2	notebook	red	green	white
3	pencil	bike	pen	eraser
4	address	phone number	bag	name
5	umbrella	book	comic	dictionary
6	TV	computer	mobile phone	ice cream

Score: ...... /5

Colour one ring on Lenny's tail for each correct answer.

My score is ....!

3 Wild world

A Foundation exercises

Vocabulary: Feelings

1 Follow the lines and complete the sentences.

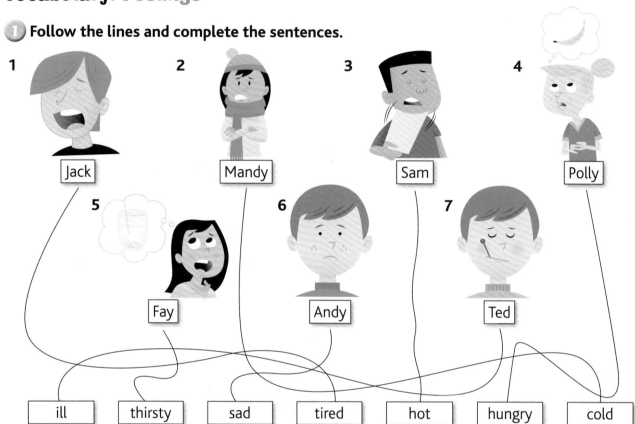

1 Jack
2 Mandy
3 Sam
4 Polly
5 Fay
6 Andy
7 Ted

ill | thirsty | sad | tired | hot | hungry | cold

1 A: What's the matter with Jack?
   B: He's _____tired_____.
2 A: What's the matter with Mandy?
   B: She's _____.
3 A: What's the matter with Sam?
   B: He's _____.
4 A: What's the matter with Polly?
   B: She's _____.

5 A: What's the matter with Fay?
   B: She's _____.
6 A: What's the matter with Andy?
   B: He's _____.
7 A: What's the matter with Ted?
   B: He's _____.

Grammar: *to be* questions

2 Look at Exercise 1. Choose the
   correct answers.

1 A: Is he hot?   **B:** No, he *is* / *isn't.*
2 A: Is she happy?   **B:** No, she *is* / *isn't.*
3 A: Is he hot?   **B:** Yes, he *is* / *isn't.*
4 A: Is she tired?   **B:** No, she *is* / *isn't.*
5 A: Is she cold?   **B:** No, she *is* / *isn't.*
6 A: Is he sad?   **B:** Yes, he *is* / *isn't.*
7 A: Is he ill?   **B:** Yes, he *is* / *isn't.*

3 Complete the questions with *Is, he*
   or *she.*

1 Is _he__ hot?   4 _____ she tired?

2 Is _____ hungry?   5 Is _____ cold?

3 _____ he sad?   6 Is _____ happy?

A Activation exercises

Vocabulary: Feelings

1 Complete the sentences.

cold   happy   hot   hungry   ill   sad
thirsty   tired

1 She's _____ill_____ .   **2** She's _____ .

3 He's _____ .   **4** He's _____ .

5 She's _____ .   **6** She's _____ .

7 He's _____ .   **8** He's _____ .

2 Complete Robbie's message.

Hi Mum! I'm at the park with Lily and Alex. Alex is ¹ 😊 ____happy____ with his football. Lily is ² 🎧 _____ and ³ 🎅 _____ . I'm ⁴ 😮 _____ ! And I'm ⁵ 😮 _____ and ⁶ 😋 _____ ! Are you at home, Mum?

Grammar: *to be* questions

3 Read and answer the questions.

Raj

I'm hungry. Here's my lunch – an apple and an orange. I'm happy now.

1 Is he ill?   _No, he isn't._
2 Is he happy now?   _____

Lily

I'm not tired, I'm ill. I'm hot and I'm not happy.

3 Is she tired?   _____
4 Is she happy?   _____

Robbie   Spot

Spot isn't sad today. He's cold and hungry!

5 Is he sad today?   _____
6 Is he cold?   _____

4 Write the words in the correct order.

1 A: he | hungry? | Is   _Is he hungry?_
B: he | No, | isn't.   _No, he isn't._

2 A: cold? | she | Is   _____
B: she | isn't. | No,   _____

3 A: she | hot? | Is   _____
B: she | Yes, | is.   _____

4 A: tired? | Is | he   _____
B: isn't. | he | No,   _____

5 A: happy? | he | Is   _____
B: is. | he | Yes,   _____

6 A: he | Is | sad?   _____
B: isn't. | he | No,   _____

5 Write questions.

1 he / cold?   _Is he cold?_
2 she / sad?   ....
3 she / tired?   ....
4 he / thirsty?   ....
5 he / hot?   ....
6 she / hungry?   ....

6 Answer the questions.

1 **A:** Is he hot?
   B: (✗ cold) _No, he isn't. He's cold._
2 **A:** Is she thirsty?
   B: (✓) _Yes, she is._
3 **A:** Is she ill?
   B: (✗ hungry) ....
4 **A:** Is she sad?
   B: (✗ ill) ....
5 **A:** Is he happy?
   B: (✗ sad) ....
6 **A:** Is he tired?
   B: (✓) ....

English today

7 Complete the dialogue. Then match the sentences with the pictures.

| about | ~~at~~ | Here | Lucky | matter | Yuck! |

a Mum: Look ¹ _at_ Hannah! She's happy now.
b Mum: What's the ² .... with Tommy?
   Hannah: He's hungry.
c Mum: ³ ....'s your lunch, Tommy.
d Tommy: Oh! ⁴ .... Prince!
e Mum: How ⁵ .... an apple, Tommy?
   Tommy: ⁶ .... No thanks!

Picture _3_
Picture ....
Picture ....
Picture ....
Picture ....

1

Tommy

2

3

Hannah

5

Prince

4

A Extension exercises

Vocabulary: Feelings

1 Complete the words.

1 h <u>o</u> <u>t</u>   **2** h _____ _____ _____ _____

3 c _____ _____ _____   **4** i _____ _____

5 s _____ _____   **6** t _____ _____ _____ _____

7 t _____ _____ _____ _____ _____   **8** h _____ _____ _____ _____

2 Write questions and answers.

1 Asha – cold
   A: *What's the matter with Asha?*
   B: *She's cold.*

2 Mrs Patel – ill
   A: _____
   B: _____

3 Mr Baker – hungry
   A: _____
   B: _____

4 Mrs Baker – thirsty
   A: _____
   B: _____

5 Raj – tired
   A: _____
   B: _____

6 Robbie – sad
   A: _____
   B: _____

Grammar: *to be* questions

3 Write questions and answers.

	Marcin	Anna	Enzo
hot			✗
tired	✓		
cold		✗	
happy			✓
hungry	✗		
thirsty		✓	

1 Marcin
   A: *Is Marcin tired?*   **B:** *Yes, he is.*
2 Marcin
   A: _____   **B:** _____
3 Anna
   A: _____   **B:** _____
4 Anna
   A: _____   **B:** _____
5 Enzo
   A: _____   **B:** _____
6 Enzo
   A: _____   **B:** _____

About you

4 Answer the questions about your family and friends.

Your friend
Name: *Peter*
Is he tired today?   *No, he isn't.*

1 Your friend
Name: _____
Is he tired today?   _____

2 Your friend
Name: _____
Is she happy today?   _____

3 A family member
Name: _____
Is _____ sad today?   _____

4 A family member
Name: _____
Is _____ today?   _____

B Foundation exercises

Vocabulary: Countries

1 Look and complete the countries.

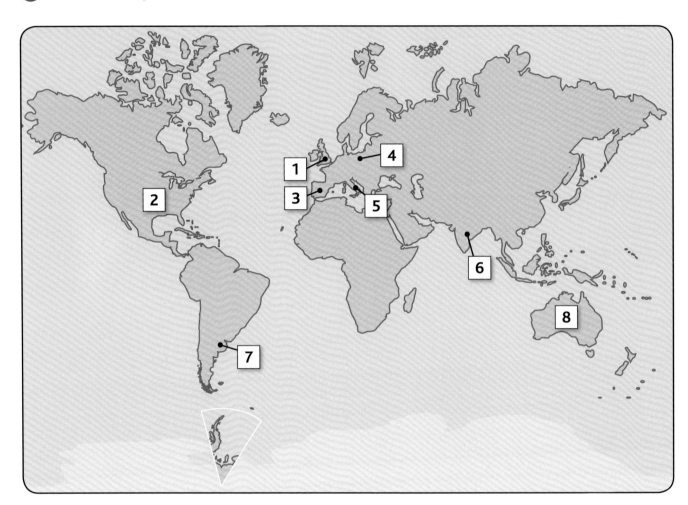

1 th_e_ U_K_
2 t_____ U_____A
3 S___a___n
4 P___l___n_____

5 It___l___
6 I____di____
7 Ar_____en____i____a
8 A_____st_____al_____a

Grammar: *to be* questions; *Where …?*

2 Complete the dialogues.

Are	~~from~~	from	they	Where	you

1 A: Where are you _from_?
   B: I'm from India.
2 A: _____ you from Australia?
   B: No, I'm not.
3 A: Are _____ from the USA?
   B: Yes, they are.

4 A: _____ are they from?
   B: They're from Spain.
5 A: Are they _____ Italy?
   B: No, they aren't.
6 A: Are _____ from Poland?
   B: No, we aren't.

Vocabulary: Countries

1 Find and write the countries.

1 .... *Italy* ....

2 ....

3 ....

4 ....

5 ....

6 ....

7 ....

8 ....

Grammar: *to be* questions; *Where ...?*

2 Complete the table.

Positive (+)	Negative (-)	Positive (+)	Negative (-)
I [1] *'m*	I'm not	We [7]	We aren't
You [2]	You aren't	You're	You [8] ....
He's	He [3]	They [9]	They [10] ....
She [4]	She isn't		
It [5]	It [6]		

3 Write the long forms.

1 we're   =   *we are*
2 we aren't   = ...
3 you're   = ...
4 you aren't   = ...
5 they're   = ...
6 they aren't   = ...

4 Complete the sentences.

are	from	~~India~~	not	They're	UK

1 We're from .... *India* ....
2 We're .... Spain.
3 I'm from the ....
4 .... from Australia.
5 Mark and Adam .... from the USA.
6 We're .... from Argentina.

5 Write the answers.

1 Where are you from?

We're from the USA.

Venus and Serena Williams,
the USA

2 Where are you from?

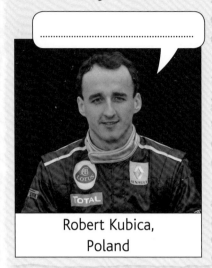

....

Robert Kubica,
Poland

3 Where are you from?

....

Shilpa Shetty and Raj
Kundra, India

4 Where are they from?

They're ....

Prince William and Kate,
the UK

5 Where are they from?

....

Hugh Jackman and Deborra-
Lee Furness, Australia

6 Where are they from?

....

Nicoletta Romanoff and
Giorgio Pasotti, Italy

6 Write questions and answers for the people in Exercise 5.

1 you / Italy?
A: *Are you from Italy?*
B: *No, we aren't.*

2 you / Spain?
A: ....
B: ....

3 you / India?
A: ....
B: ....

4 they / Poland?
A: ....
B: ....

5 they / Australia?
A: ....
B: ....

6 they / the UK?
A: ....
B: ....

7 Put the sentences in the correct order.

a Larry: Hi! I'm Larry. What's your name? [1]

b Gemma: I'm from Australia. Where are
you from? ☐

c Gemma: Hello, I'm Gemma. ☐

d Gemma: Really? Cool! ☐

e Larry: I'm from the UK. My grandparents
are from Australia, too. ☐

f Larry: Where are you from? ☐

B Extension exercises

Vocabulary: Countries

1 Match the letters to make eight countries.

| 1 ARGEN | 2 IT | 3 SP | 4 IND |
| 5 THE U | 6 POL | 7 AUSTR | 8 THE |

| AND | SA | UK | AIN |
| ALIA | ALY | TINA | IA |

1 _Argentina_   3 ....   5 ....   7 ....
2 ....   4 ....   6 ....   8 ....

Grammar: *to be* questions; *Where ...?*

2 Write dialogues. Interview the stars.

1 Katy Perry | the UK ✗ | the USA ✓ |

You: *Hi Katy! Where are you from? Are you from the UK?*

Katy: *No, I'm not. I'm from the USA!*

2 Robert Pattinson | Poland ✗ | the UK ✓ |

You: ....

Robert: ....

3 Rafael Nadal | Argentina ✗ | Spain ✓ |

You: ....

Rafael: ....

4 Emma Watson | the USA ✗ | the UK ✓ |

You: ....

Emma: ....

5 Cesc Fàbregas | The UK ✗ | Spain ✓ |

You: ....

Cesc: ....

6 Miley Cyrus | Italy ✗ | the USA ✓ |

You: ....

Miley: ....

3 Write questions and answers about the stars in Exercise 2.

1 Katy and Miley
Where _are they_ from?
They're _from the USA._

2 Rafael and Cesc
....
....

3 Robert and Emma
....
....

About you

4 Write to Gosia about your family.

Gosia's blog

Hi, my name's Gosia. This is my mum. Her name's Justyna. Here's my dad. His name's Bartek. We're from Poland. Where are you from?

....
....
....

C Foundation exercises

Vocabulary: Wild animals

1 Look and choose the correct words.

1 It's *a crocodile /* (a zebra).

2 It's *an ostrich / an elephant.*

3 It's *a giraffe / a monkey.*

4 It's *a parrot / a snake.*

5 It's *a lion / an ostrich.*

6 It's *a monkey / a snake.*

Grammar: Plural nouns; *our / their*

2 Complete the words. Write *s* or *es*.

One	Two or more
1 elephant	elephant *s*
2 lion	lion .....
3 ostrich	ostrich .....
4 monkey	monkey .....
5 snake	snake .....
6 crocodile	crocodile .....

3 Complete the sentences with *our* or *their*.

1 Look at __*their*__ photos!

2 This is .... computer.

3 She's their mother.

4 It's .... TV.

5 He's .... father.

6 Here's .... lunch.

C Activation exercises

Vocabulary: Wild animals

1 Find the correct stickers.

1 It's a parrot.

2 It's a snake.

3 It's an elephant.

4 It's an ostrich.

5 It's a polar bear.

6 It's a lion.

2 Match the letters to make six animal words. Then write.

1	ele	rich	1	*elephant*
2	croco	affe	2	....
3	gir	bra	3	....
4	ost	phant	4	....
5	mon	key	5	....
6	ze	dile	6	....

Grammar: Plural nouns; *our / their*

3 **2 50** Listen and number the pictures.

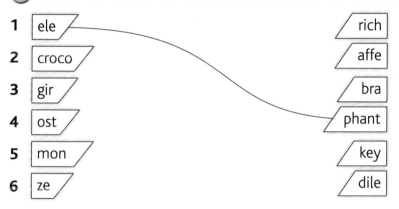

A ☐

B ☐

C ☐

D ☐

E 1

F ☐

4 Write the plurals.

1 one elephant
three ..... *elephants* .....

2 one parrot
five ....

3 one ostrich
two ....

4 one polar bear
four ....

5 one crocodile
six ....

6 one giraffe
three ....

5 Complete the sentences with *our* or *their*.

1 The penguins are hungry. Here's ..*their*.. lunch.

2 I'm Robbie and Alex is my brother. Lily is .... sister.

3 Raj and Asha are brother and sister. Sanjay is .... dad.

4 The monkeys are cute – look at .... faces!

5 Harry is my friend. We're in class 2. Mrs Green is .... teacher.

6 Look at the crocodiles – .... bodies are long!

6 Complete the text with *our* or *their*.

Land of the Lemurs

Woburn Safari Park is a big zoo in the UK.

What's 'Land of the Lemurs'? It's a new home for the lemurs. They're very happy in ¹ ..*their*.. new home.

The lemurs are ² .... favourite animals here at the zoo. They're cute! ³ .... bodies are grey, and ⁴ .... faces are black and white.

Meet ⁵ .... lemurs and ⁶ .... zookeepers here at Woburn Safari Park!

7 Read the text again and answer *True* (✓) or *False* (x).

1 Woburn Safari Park is a small zoo. [x]
2 It's in the UK. [ ]
3 'Land of the Lemurs' isn't new. [ ]
4 'Land of the Lemurs' is a home for the lemurs. [ ]
5 Lemurs aren't cute. [ ]
6 Lemurs are green and white. [ ]

Vocabulary: Wild animals

1 **What animals are they from?**

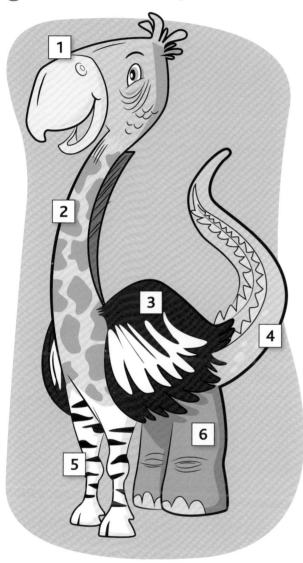

1	_a parrot_	4	....
2	....	5	....
3	....	6	....

Grammar: Plural nouns; *our / their*

2 **Write the plurals.**

1 one book   two _books_
2 one elephant two ....
3 one pen   three ....
4 one ostrich   two ....
5 one bag   three ....
6 one zebra   four ....

3 **Complete the dialogue.**

My	~~our~~	our	their	their	their

Zookeeper: Look at [1] _our_ parrots.
Robbie: Wow! What colour are [2] .... bodies?
Zookeeper: They're red and blue.
Robbie: And [3] .... faces are green and yellow. Cool!
Zookeeper: Now, meet [4] .... snakes!
Lily: Snakes? Yuck!
Zookeeper: No, no. Look, [5] .... faces are cute. They're amazing animals.
Robbie: Snakes aren't cute. [6] .... sister is cute.
Lily: Thanks, Robbie!

About you

4 **What's in your bag? Draw pictures and write.**
Two books
Three pens

Check

1 Choose the correct words to complete the text.

Tara's hungry!

Jared is a zookeeper. His ¹ _animals_ are the parrots and ... the elephants!

- ² .... are the parrots from, Jared?

Jared: ³ .... *from Australia.* ⁴ .... *colours are amazing — red, blue, yellow and green.*

- They're great. And where are the elephants from? Are they from India?

Jared: *Yes, they are.*

- Look at that elephant. ⁵ .... her name?

Jared: *Her name's Tara.*

- ⁶ .... Tara hungry?

Jared: *Yes, she is. Tara, here's an apple!*

- Cool!

Jared

1 A books	**B** animals	**C** countries		**4 A** My	**B** Their	**C** Our
2 A Where	**B** Who	**C** What		**5 A** What's	**B** Who's	**C** Where's
3 A It's	**B** We're	**C** They're		**6 A** Are	**B** Is	**C** Am

Score: ...... /5

2 Write the words in the correct columns.

cold   crocodile   ~~giraffe~~   Poland   thirsty   the UK

Colour one ring on Lenny's tail for each correct answer.

My score is ....!

36

4 In my room

A Foundation exercises

Vocabulary: Clothes

1 Look and write the clothes words.

1 *trainers*

2 ....

3 ....

4 ....

5 ....

6 ....

Grammar: Possessive 's

2 Complete the sentences.

| David   Emma   Jack   Peter   Rosie   ~~Sara~~ |

1 It's S*ara's* bag.

2 It's E.............. pen.

3 It's P.............. notebook.

4 It's D.............. jacket.

5 It's R.............. mobile phone.

6 It's J.............. ruler.

A Activation exercises

Vocabulary: Clothes

1 Write the letters in the correct order.
Then match the words with the pictures.

1 krtsi   _skirt_   **3** esosh   ....

2 sdesr   ....   **4** orseusrt   ....

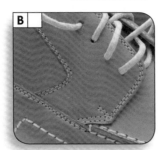

2 Find ten clothes words. Write them below.

.....jeans.....
....
....
....
....
....
....
....
....
....

O	D	J	E	A	N	S	D
K	U	G	M	P	E	K	J
L	T	A	J	B	V	I	C
T	R	O	U	S	E	R	S
E	A	K	M	O	J	T	R
N	I	M	P	F	D	Q	I
F	N	V	E	Z	R	U	J
W	E	S	R	P	E	X	A
Y	R	I	F	T	S	T	C
K	S	H	O	E	S	W	K
D	R	A	L	F	P	U	E
U	E	T	S	H	I	R	T

3 Complete the clothes words.

1 These are my t _r_ ai _n_ e _r_ _s_.
2 It's her red d .... ss.
3 This is my j ..... m .... r.
4 That's your ..... -s .... rt.
5 These are my blue ..... e ..... ns.
6 It's a black j .... k ..... t.

Grammar: Possessive 's

4 Find the correct stickers and
write sentences.

1 **Lottie:** My T-shirt is red.
This is _Lottie's T-shirt_ .

2 **Holly:** My hat is blue.
This is ....

3 **Simon:** My shoes are black.
These are ....

4 **Jenny:** My T-shirt is yellow.
This is ....

5 **Harry:** My hat is white.
This is ....

6 **Kyle:** My shoes are brown.
These are ....

Grammar: *this / these*

5 Complete the sentences with *This is* or
These are.

1 .....This is..... Dad's chair.
2 .... Robbie's jeans.
3 .... Raj's phone.
4 .... Asha's bedroom.
5 .... Alex's shoes.
6 .... Lily's trainers.

English today

6 **Complete the dialogue.**

| I don't know   No way! |

Mum: Are these your trainers, Alex?
Alex: ¹ .... They're pink!
Mum: Where are your trainers?
Alex: ² ...., Mum. Sorry!

7 **Look and answer the questions.**

Miley Cyrus

Naomi Watts

Will Smith

Justin Bieber

1 What's this?
It's Naomi's jacket.

2 What are these?
....

3 What are these?
....

4 What's this?
....

A Extension exercises

Vocabulary: Clothes

1 **Find the names and write sentences.**

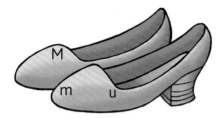

1 They're ....*Mum's shoes*.......... .

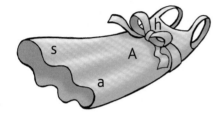

2 It's ....

3 These are ....

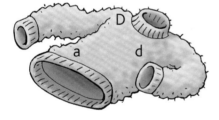

4 This is ....

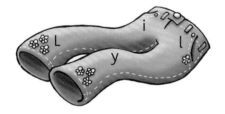

5 They're ....

6 It's ....

About you

2 **You are Sarah or Jamal. Write about your favourite clothes.**

Sarah

Jamal

My favourite clothes

This is me in my favourite clothes. This is my favourite ....

....

....

....

....

3 **Think about your family and/or friends. Write about their favourite things.**

My mum's favourite thing is her phone. It's blue. Her favourite clothes are her red jumper and her yellow trainers.

1 ....

....

....

2 ....

....

....

3 ....

....

B Foundation exercises

Vocabulary: Rooms and furniture

1 Look and write the words.

bath   chair   ~~cooker~~   cupboard   sofa   table

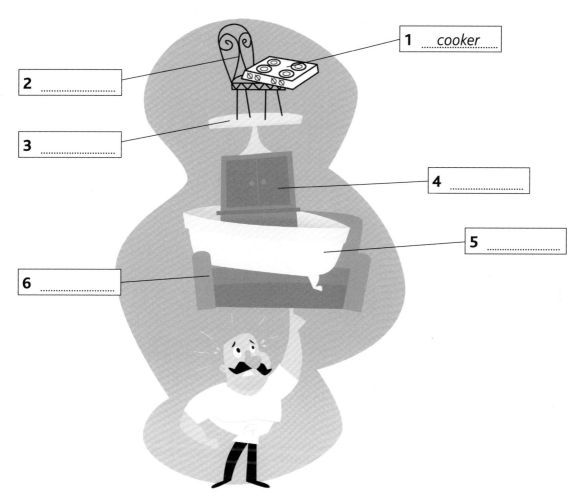

1   _cooker_

2   ....

3   ....

4   ....

5   ....

6   ....

Grammar: in, on, under

2 Write *in*, *on* or *under*.

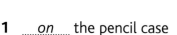

1   ..._on_... the pencil case

2   .... the pencil case

3   .... the pencil case

3 Look at the picture in Exercise 1. Choose the correct words.

1   The table is *in / on / under* the chair.
2   The cooker is *in / on / under* the chair.
3   The chair is *in / on / under* the cooker.

4   The chair is *in / on / under* the table.
5   The cupboard is *in / on / under* the bath.
6   The sofa is *in / on / under* the bath.

B Activation exercises

Vocabulary: Rooms and furniture

1 Find and write the rooms.

g o i r ~~v n i l o m~~

b r m d o e o

1 ___living room___

2 _____

k i c n t e h

r b m t o a h o

3 _____

4 _____

2 Complete the crossword.

1

7

2

6

3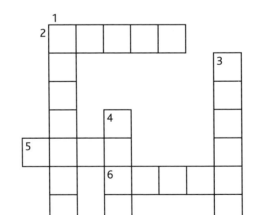

4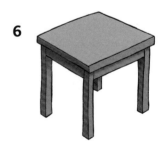

5

Grammar: *in, on, under*

3 **Choose and write the correct word.**

1 Where's my jacket? It's ___in___ the cupboard.

    A under   **B** in

2 Where are Alex and Lily? They're _____ the classroom.

    A in   **B** on

3 Where are my jeans? They're _____ the chair.

    A on   **B** in

4 Where's my pen? It's _____ my pencil case.

    A on   **B** in

5 Where's Mum? She's _____ the kitchen.

    A under   **B** in

6 Where's Spot? He's _____ the table.

    A in   **B** under

4 **Complete the rap.**

Here	In	In	On	~~Under~~	where's

Ring ring, where's the phone?

Ring ring, where's the phone?

¹ _Under_ the bed? No, no!

² _____ the bathroom? No, no!

Ring ring, ³ _____ the phone?

Ring ring, where's the phone?

⁴ _____ the kitchen? Yes, yes!

⁵ _____ the table? Yes, yes!

Ring ring, RING RING!

⁶ _____ it is! ... Hello?

About you

5 **Write about your home.**

1 Where's the bath? _It's in the bathroom._

2 Where's your bed? _____

3 Where's the TV? _____

4 Where's the cooker? _____

5 Where's the sofa? _____

6 Where's the phone? _____

6 ②51 **Listen and tick (✓) the correct picture.**

1 ☐

2 ☐

3 ☐

English today

7 **Match the pictures with the phrases. There is one extra picture.**

1 Here I come! ......

2 Don't be silly! ......

B Extension exercises

Vocabulary: Rooms and furniture

1 Complete the sentences.

1

Benny

Benny's cooker *is in the bedroom* .

2

Macy

.... bed ....

3

Lenny

.... books ....

4

Stacey

.... skateboard ....

5

Kenny

.... clothes ....

6

Lacey

.... computer ....

2 Use the code to find the message.

A	B	C	D	E
Z	Y	X	W	V
F	**G**	**H**	**I**	**J**
U	T	S	R	Q
K	**L**	**M**	**N**	**O**
P	O	N	M	L
P	**Q**	**R**	**S**	**T**
K	J	I	H	G
U	**V**	**W**	**X**	**Y**
F	E	D	C	B
Z				
A				

NB UZELFIRGV ILLN RH NB YVWILLN.
DSZG'H BLFI UZELFIRGV ILLN?

My ....
....

3 Read the text and answer the questions.

> My favourite room is my bedroom.
> My computer is on the table. My bag and
> my books are on the bed. My clothes are in
> the cupboard and my phone is in the bed!
>
> Joseph

1 What is Joseph's favourite room?
  His favourite room is his bedroom. ....
2 Where are Joseph's books? ....
3 Is his phone on the table? ....
4 Where's his bag? ....
5 Are Joseph's jeans on the bed? (Think!)

....

About you

4 Write about your favourite room. Use Exercise 3 to help you.

My favourite room is ....
....
....
....
....

Speaking: Look for things

1 **Complete the dialogue.**

At the swimming pool.

Lucy: Where's my phone? Oh no! Where is it?

Pia: ¹ *What's it like?*

Lucy: It's small and red.

Pia: Is it in your bag?

Lucy: ² .... It's lost!

Pia: Is it ³ ....?

Lucy: I don't know.

Pia Look, Lucy. ⁴ .... It's under your bag!

Lucy: Oh, ⁵ ....!

Pia: You're ⁶ ....

> No, it isn't.
> welcome
> thank you
> in your jacket
> ~~What's it like?~~
> There it is.

Your turn

2 **Put the dialogue in the correct order. Use Exercise 1 to help you.**

Dad and James are in the bedroom.

a Dad: You're welcome. [8]

b James: Where's my jacket? Oh no! Where is it? [1]

c Dad: Look, James. There it is. It's under your bed! ☐

d James: Oh, thank you! ☐

e Dad: Is it in your cupboard? ☐

f James: It's green. ☐

g James: No, it isn't. It's lost! ☐

h Dad: What's it like? ☐

3 **Write the dialogue in your notebook.**

Writing: Find a lost pet

4 **Answer the questions about Jack's pet.**

What animal is Jack's pet?	dog
What's the problem?	lost
What's his name?	Shane
How old is Shane?	two
What's Shane like?	big and black
What's Jack's phone number?	1692 0368542

1 What's Jack's problem? *His dog is lost.* ....

2 What's the dog's name? ....

3 What colour is the dog? ....

4 Is he a small dog? ....

Your turn

5 **Write a poster to find Jack's pet. Use the poster on page 41 of your Student's Book to help you.**

LOST! SHANE

This ....*is Shane*....... .

He's .... and he's lost.

.... years old.

He's .... and black.

Please find ....

Thank you!

Phone me on ....

Check

1 **Choose the correct words to complete the text.**

Kylie's blog

Welcome to my favourite room [1] *in* the house: my [2] ....! My favourite things in my room are my posters, my TV (it isn't in the picture) and my [3] ....! Today my clothes aren't in the cupboard – they're [4] .... the bed! [5] .... are my favourite clothes – my blue and white [6] .... from Italy, and my red trainers. What are your favourite clothes?

1 A under	**B** on	**C** (in)	
2 A sofa	**B** bedroom	**C** chair	
3 A bed	**B** cooker	**C** bath	

4 A in	**B** on	**C** under	
5 A These	**B** This	**C** It	
6 A kitchen	**B** jacket	**C** phone	

Score: ...... /5

2 **Write the words in the correct columns.**

bed   cupboard   ~~dress~~   kitchen   living room   trousers

Clothes	Rooms	Things in the rooms
dress		

Score: ...... /5

Colour one ring on Lenny's tail for each correct answer.

My score is ....!

5 People and pets

A Foundation exercises

Vocabulary: Possessions (2)

1 Look and write the words.

| a CD player   an MP3 player   a pair of sunglasses   a sleeping bag   a tent   ~~a torch~~   a watch |

1 *a torch*

2 ....

3 ....

4 ....

5 ....

6 ....

7 ....

Grammar: have got

2 Read and complete.

| I've/I ¹ *haven't* | got a watch. |
| You've/You ² .... | |

| Have you ³ .... a tent? | Yes, I have./No, I ⁴ .... |

3 Complete the sentences.

| got   Have   haven't   haven't   ~~'ve~~   You |

1 I *'ve* got a pair of sunglasses.
2 ....'ve got a watch.
3 A: .... you got a torch?
   B: Yes, I have.

4 I haven't .... a CD player.
5 You .... got a torch.
6 A: Have you got a CD player?
   B: No, I ....

A Activation exercises

Vocabulary: Possessions (2)

1 Look and complete Tilly's sentences.

1 I've got _____ *sunglasses* _____ .
2 I've got _____ .
3 I've got _____ .
4 I've got _____ .
5 I've got _____ .
6 I've got _____ .
7 I've got _____ .

Grammar: *have got*

2 Write questions for Tilly.

1 (torch) *Have you got a torch?* _____

2 (computer) _____

3 (skateboard) _____

4 (TV) _____

5 (bike) _____

6 (dog) _____

3 Make the sentences negative.

1   I've got a dog.
  (✗)   *I haven't got a dog.* _____

2   You've got an MP3 player.
  (✗) _____

3   You've got a football shirt.
  (✗) _____

4   I've got an umbrella.
  (✗) _____

5   You've got a sleeping bag.
  (✗) _____

6   I've got a computer.
  (✗) _____

4 Write the words in the correct order.

1 [brother.] [got] [a] [You've]
You've got a brother.

2 [haven't] [I] [sister.] [got] [a]
....

3 [CD player.] [a] [haven't] [got] [You]
....

4 [a] [got] [pair] [I've] [sunglasses.] [of]
....

5 [got] [a] [You've] [camera.]
....

6 [I] [a] [haven't] [got] [jacket.]
....

5 Write sentences.

1 I / (✓) torch / (✗) MP3 player
I've got a torch. I haven't got an MP3 player.

2 You / (✓) bike / (✗) TV
....

3 I / (✗) dog / (✓) parrot
....

4 You / (✓) apple / (✗) ice cream
....

5 I / (✗) brother / (✓) sister
....

6 You / (✓) bed / (✗) sofa
....

About you

6 Write answers about you.

1 Have you got an MP3 player?
Yes, I have./No, I haven't.

2 Have you got a brother?
....

3 Have you got a tent?
....

4 Have you got a pet?
....

5 Have you got an apple?
....

6 Have you got your trainers today?
....

English today

7 Complete the speech bubbles.

Here you are.   ~~Oh no, it's broken!~~
Let me look.   Typical!

1

2

3

A Extension exercises

Vocabulary: Possessions (2)

1) **Look and write the words.**

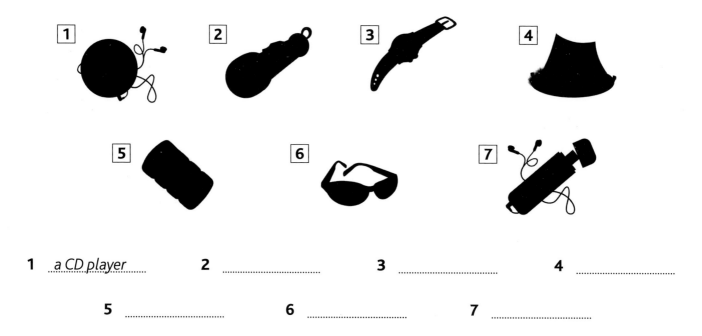

1 *a CD player*   2 .... 3 .... 4 ....

     5 .... 6 .... 7 ....

Grammar: *have got*

2) **Complete the email with *'ve got, haven't got* or *Have … got*.**

Hi!

I'm Ewa. I'm from Poland. Where are you from? It's my birthday today. I'm eleven. How old are you? I got an MP3 player for my birthday! ☺ ¹ ...*Have*... you ...*got*... an MP3 player?

I ² .... two brothers but I ³ .... a sister ☹. ⁴ .... you .... brothers or sisters?

My favourite thing is my mobile phone. It's pink! ⁵ .... you .... a mobile phone? What colour is it?

Bye!

Ewa

About you

3) **Write an email to Ewa about you. Answer Ewa's questions from Exercise 2.**

Hi Ewa!

I'm from .... I'm .... years old.

....

....

....

....

....

....

Bye!

B Foundation exercises

5

Vocabulary: Appearance

1 Complete the appearance words.

1 b _r_ o _w_ n   3 l ..... ng   5 gr ..... e .....
2 bl ..... n ..... e   4 b ..... u .....   6 r ..... d

2 Match the words with the pictures.

| black   blonde   ~~brown~~   long   short   ~~medium-length~~   short   blonde |

1

medium-length
brown

2

3

4

Grammar: *have got*

3 Choose the correct words.

1 He ⓢ / 've got short black hair.
2 He *'s* / *'ve* got red hair.
3 He *haven't* / *hasn't* got black eyes.
4 She *haven't* / *hasn't* got brown eyes.
5 She *hasn't* / *haven't* got blonde hair.
6 She *'s* / *'ve* got medium-length hair.

4 Complete the questions and answers. Write *'s*, *has* or *hasn't*.

1 **A:** _Has_ he got long brown hair?
  B: No, he _hasn't_ .
2 **A:** What kind of hair .... she got?
  B: She .... got long red hair.
3 **A:** What kind of hair .... he got?
  B: He .... got short brown hair.
4 **A:** .... he got grey eyes?
  B: No, he ....
5 **A:** .... she got long hair?
  B: No, she ....
6 **A:** .... he got green eyes?
  B: No, he ....

51

B Activation exercises

Vocabulary: Appearance

1 **Find ten appearance words. Write them below.**

B	L	A	C	K	R	W	K	M
R	D	C	L	O	N	G	L	E
M	V	J	S	R	A	R	E	D
T	I	D	B	L	U	E	M	I
Y	J	G	L	S	M	Y	V	U
O	B	R	O	W	N	E	N	M
D	E	E	N	Y	O	A	F	L
U	T	E	D	F	H	I	O	E
Q	L	N	E	E	A	H	L	N
P	E	D	X	L	U	Y	T	G
C	W	O	M	S	H	O	R	T
B	E	M	A	E	T	P	I	H

......*red*...... ....

....

....

....

....

2 **Choose the correct words.**

1 She's got *green / grey* hair.
2 He's got *blue / blonde* eyes.
3 She hasn't got *glasses / eyes*.
4 He's got *short / blue* hair.
5 She's got *short / green* eyes.
6 He's got *black / long* glasses.

3 **Read, draw and colour.**

This is my sister, Alison. She's got medium-length red hair and green eyes. She hasn't got glasses.

English today

4 **Complete the dialogue.**

called	Excuse me	Phew!

Sadie: Mr Green, my pet dog is lost.

Mr Green: What colour is he?

Sadie: He's brown and white.

Mrs White: ¹ ...., here's a dog. He's ² .... Archie. Is he your dog?

Sadie: Archie! Yes, that's my dog! ³ .... Thank you.

Grammar: *have got*

5 **Read the descriptions and find the correct stickers.**

1 He's got short black hair.
2 She's got long blonde hair.
3 He's got medium-length red hair.
4 She's got long brown hair.

1 [image]   2 [ ]

3 [ ]   4 [ ]

6 **Complete the sentences with *'s got* or *hasn't got*.**

1 (✗) Alex ...*hasn't got*... long hair.
2 (✗) Lily .... grey hair.
3 (✓) Mr Patel .... brown eyes.
4 (✓) Mr Baker .... short hair.
5 (✗) Asha .... blue eyes.
6 (✓) Raj .... black hair.

7 Look and write the questions and answers.

black hair

brown eyes

Sandeep

blonde hair

green eyes

Will

red hair

blue eyes

Sarah

1 Blue eyes?
  A: *Has he got blue eyes?*
  B: *No, he hasn't.*

2 Black hair?
  A: ....
  B: ....

3 Red hair?
  A: ....
  B: ....

4 Green eyes?
  A: ....
  B: ....

5 Long hair?
  A: ....
  B: ....

6 Brown eyes?
  A: ....
  B: ....

8 Describe the people in Exercise 7.

Sandeep
He's got medium-length black hair and brown eyes. He hasn't got glasses.

Will
....
....
....
....

Sarah
....
....
....
....

9 Describe Elizabeth Swann and Peter Parker.

	Elizabeth Swann (Keira Knightley)	Peter Parker (Tobey Maguire)
Hair colour	blonde	brown
Hair length	long	short
Eye colour	brown	blue
Glasses?	no	yes

1 Elizabeth Swann
  She's got ....
....
....

2 Peter Parker
....
....
....

B Extension exercises

Vocabulary: Appearance

1 Write the words in the correct columns.

| black | blonde | blue | brown | green | grey | long | medium-length | red | short |

Hair colour	Hair length	Eye colour
black		

Grammar: *have got*

2 Read the text and answer the questions.

My favourite star is Adam G. Sevani. He's from the USA. He's nineteen. He hasn't got short hair – he's got medium-length black hair and he's got big brown eyes. He hasn't got glasses. He's nice! He's got a brother called Vahe. Vahe is twenty-three.

1 What's his name?   *His name's Adam G. Sevani.*
2 Where's he from?
3 How old is he?
4 What kind of hair has he got?
5 What colour are his eyes?
6 Has he got glasses?
7 Has he got a brother?
8 What's his brother's name?
9 How old is Vahe?

About you

3 Describe your favourite actor or singer. Find a picture.

C Foundation exercises

Vocabulary: Pets; Parts of animals

1 **What animal is it? Look and write the animals.**

| bird | ~~cat~~ | dog | fish | hamster | lizard | rabbit | tortoise |

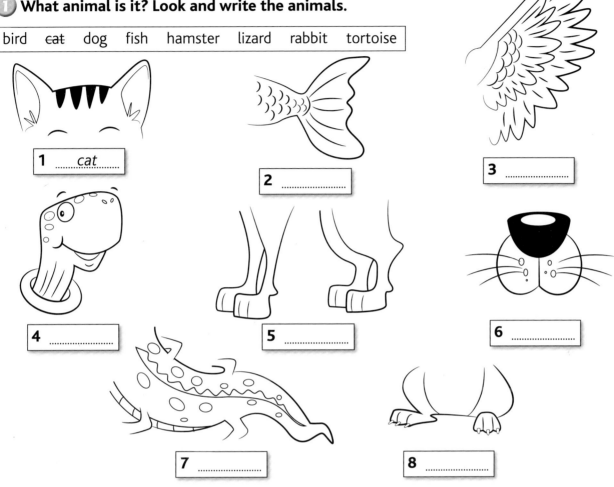

1 _cat_

2 ....

3 ....

4 ....

5 ....

6 ....

7 ....

8 ....

2 **Complete the words. They are all parts of animals.**

1 e _a_ rs
2 ta l
3 wi ..... g
4 h ..... ad
5 l ..... gs and pa ..... s
6 n ..... se
7 bod .....
8 fe ..... t

Grammar: _have got_

3 **Complete the sentences with 've, have, haven't or got.**

1 (✓) The cats ..... _have_ ..... got long tails.
2 (✗) We haven't .... dogs.
3 (✗) We .... got a garden.
4 (✓) We .... got three cats.
5 (?) .... the cats got short legs?
6 (✗) No, they ....!

4 **Complete the table.**

+	-	?
I ..... _'ve_ ..... got ...	I _haven't_ got ...	..... _Have_ ..... I got ... ?
You .... got ...	You haven't	Have .... got ... ?
He .... got ...	He hasn't got ...	Has .... got ... ?
She's	She .... got ...	.... she got ... ?
We .... got ...	We haven't	Have .... got ... ?
They've	They .... got ...	Have .... got ... ?

C Activation exercises

Vocabulary: Pets; Parts of animals

1 Find and write the animals.

1 atc .... *cat* .....
2 dbri ....
3 sfhi ....
4 gdo ....
5 zdrlia ....
6 emsrhat ....
7 rtoetosi ....

2 Correct the sentences.

1 It's an ear.
  No, it's a tail. .....

2 It's a head.
  ....

3 They're wings.
  ....

4 They're paws.
  ....

5 It's a head.
  ....

6 It's a leg.
  ....

3 Look at the pictures in Exercise 2. Write the animal and the part of the animal.

1 *It's a fish's tail.* ....
2 ....
3 ....
4 ....
5 ....
6 ....

English today

4 Complete the dialogue.

| lots of   Maybe   not sure |

Pattie: Look, Mum! They've got ¹ .... cats here.

Freddie: Mum, we've got a dog but we haven't got a cat. Mum, please ...

Mum: Two pets? I'm ² ....

Freddie: Mum, please. Look, this cat is very friendly.

Mum: ³ .... next year.

F and P: OK, Mum!

Grammar: *have got*

5 🔊 52 Listen and tick (✓).

		Yes	No
1	Tom has got three sisters.	☐	✓
2	Tom's family has got lots of pets.	☐	☐
3	Snowy has got brown ears.	☐	☐
4	Alfie has got a white body.	☐	☐
5	Tom has got a pet lizard.	☐	☐
6	Tom's pet has got a short tail.	☐	☐

6 Write sentences.

1 long tails

We've got long tails.

They've got long tails.

2 big heads

3 short legs

4 little noses

5 long ears

6 big paws

7 Look at the pictures in Exercise 6. Write questions and answers about them.

1 short tails? *Have they got short tails?*
No, they haven't.

2 big heads?

3 short legs?

4 big noses?

5 short ears?

6 big paws?

8 Complete the text with *'ve got, have got, haven't got* or *Have you got*.

Name	Nicholas Clark
Address	Grasstown Farm, Somerset, UK
Family	Jake (dad), Claire (mum), Sam (brother)
Pets	Two rabbits, two hamsters, five fish, three dogs

My name's Nicholas and I ¹ *'ve got* a brother, Sam. Our parents ² .... a farm. We ³ .... lots of pets. We ⁴ .... rabbits, hamsters, fish and dogs but we ⁵ .... cats. ⁶ .... a pet?

C Extension exercises

Vocabulary: Pets; Parts of animals

1 **Look and write sentences.**

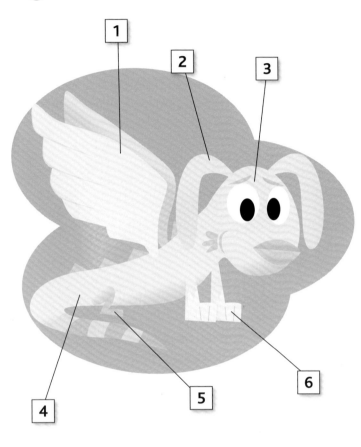

1 *It's got a bird's wings.*
2 *It's got a rabbit's ears.*
3 ....
4 ....
5 ....
6 ....

Grammar: *have got*

2 **Write sentences. Use the correct form of *have / has got*.**

1 we / two dogs   *We've got two dogs.*
2 Peter / a pet lizard ....
3 my dog / not / a long tail ....
4 you / a tortoise? ....?
5 I / not / a pet fish ....
6 your dog / a black nose? ....?

3 **Complete the text with the correct form of *have got*.**

Hi! My name's Andrea. I ¹ *'ve got* two brothers, Marc and Paul. We ² .... two dogs and a cat, and we ³ .... a big garden at home – it's great for the pets! Our dogs' names are Scampi and Chips. They're brown and black and they ⁴ .... short legs! Our cat ⁵ .... white paws and a long black tail. She ⁶ .... a black nose. Her name is L.C. (that's Little Cat). She's very friendly. ⁷ .... you .... a pet?

4 **Read the text in Exercise 3. Answer the questions.**

1 Has Andrea got two sisters?
   No, she hasn't.
2 Have they got four pets?
   ....
3 Have they got a big garden?
   ....
4 Have the dogs got long legs?
   ....
5 Has the cat got white paws?
   ....
6 Has she got a long tail?
   ....

About you

5 **Write about your pet or a friend's pet. Use Exercise 3 to help you.**

Hi! My name's / friend's name is ....
....
....
....
....
....

1 Read the text and answer the questions.

Shelley's blog

Here is my family. Where am I? Look! I've got long blonde hair. My sister's name is Hayley. She's got long brown hair. We've got a dog called Alesha. She's black and white and has got a long tail. She's very friendly. Mum's got long red hair and green eyes. My dad is in the photo. He's got short brown hair. We've got a tent and four sleeping bags. We haven't got beds and we haven't got a TV but it's cool.

1 What kind of hair has Shelley got?   *She's got long blonde hair.*

2 What's her sister's name?   ....

3 Who's Alesha?   ....

4 Has she got a short tail?   ....

5 What kind of hair has Shelley's dad got?   ....

6 Have they got a TV?   ....

Score: ...... /5

2 Which word is different? Choose.

Number one is 'fish' (CD player, MP3 player and watch are objects)

1 CD player	MP3 player	watch	(fish)
2 short	torch	long	medium-length
3 nose	tail	paw	tortoise
4 black	hamster	lizard	bird
5 blonde	grey	glasses	black
6 red	green	long	brown

Score: ...... /5

Colour one ring on Lenny's tail for each correct answer.

My score is ....!

6 Action!

A Foundation exercises

Vocabulary: Action verbs

1 Look and complete the sentences.

| Close | eat | laugh | ~~Open~~ | run | Stop! |

1 ...... *Open* ...... the door.

2 Don't ....!

3 Don't .... in class.

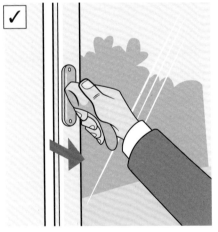

4 .... the window.

5 ....

6 Don't ....!

2 Choose the correct words.

1 (Open)/ *Listen* the window.

2 *Stand / Stop* up!

3 Don't *eat / close* here!

4 *Sit / Laugh* down.

5 *Eat / Listen* to me.

6 Don't *laugh / open*!

Grammar: Giving instructions

3 Find and write the missing words to complete the sentences.

1 Don't (nru) .... *run* ....!

2 (datnS) .... up.

3 (loCes) .... the door.

4 (ieLsnt) .... to me.

5 Don't (tpso) ....

6 Sit (odnw) ....

A Activation exercises

Vocabulary: Action verbs

1 Choose the correct words.

1 Close the (door) / apple.

2 Listen to the teacher / chair.

3 Open the laugh / window.

4 Eat your ice cream / trousers.

5 Sit stop / down!

6 Don't run in the classroom / talk.

2 Complete the words.

1 S _i_ t on the chair.

2 Don't l .... h at me.

3 S .... p! Don't run in school.

4 Sm .... e for the photo.

5 St .... d ..... p! Your teacher is here.

6 T .... k to your friends.

English today

3 Complete the dialogue.

Excellent.   let's start again   we're ready

Miss Carr: OK everyone?

Robbie: Yes, Miss Carr, [1] ....

Miss Carr: Lily, where are you?

Lily: Here, Miss Carr!

Miss Carr: [2] .... Sit down, Lily.
Oh, where's Raj?

Raj: I'm here!

Miss Carr: Good. Now, [3] .... ,
everyone!

Grammar: Giving instructions

4 Make these instructions negative.

1 Run! (✗) _Don't run!_

2 Talk! (✗) ....

3 Eat! (✗) ....

4 Sit down! (✗) ....

5 Laugh! (✗) ....

6 Stop! (✗) ....

5 Match the instructions with the pictures.

Close the window!   Don't eat here.   ~~Stop!~~   Don't run!   Don't talk!   Listen to me.

1 _Stop!_ ....

2 ....

3 ....

4 ....

5 ....

6 ....

6 Match the parts of the dialogues.

1 I'm hot.
2 Where's my chair?
3 I'm tired.
4 Here's the teacher.
5 I'm hungry.
6 Look at Robbie's helmet! Ha ha!

a Sit down.
b Don't laugh.
c Eat a sandwich.
d Open the window.
e Don't talk now.
f Here it is. Sit down.

7 Complete the dialogue.

be   laugh   ~~Sit~~
stand   talk   walk

Stefan: We're ready, Angela. ¹ _Sit_ down here. Now, don't ² .... happy. You're sad in this film.

Angela: Sorry, Mr Peelberg.

Stefan: OK, Angela, ³ .... up and ⁴ .... to the window.

Angela: Is this OK?

Stefan: Yes, but ⁵ .... to the dog, Angela!

Angela: Sorry! OK ... 'My little dog, you're my friend.' Ha! Ha! Ha!

Stefan: Angela, don't ⁶ .... What's the matter?

Angela: The dog is really funny in his jumper! Ha ha!

8 Write the words in the correct order. Then write the school rules in the poster below.

1 teacher. to Listen your
   Listen to your teacher.

2 your Talk to in English. friends
   ....

3 classroom. eat in Don't the
   ....

4 run Don't school. in
   ....

5 homework your Do in evening. the
   ....

6 class. be Don't silly in
   ....

SCHOOL RULES

YES

Listen to your teacher. ....

....

....

NO

....

....

....

A Extension exercises

Vocabulary: Action verbs

1 Match the words to make six instructions. Then write.

1	7	*Close the bathroom door.*
☐	☐	....
☐	☐	....
☐	☐	....
☐	☐	....
☐	☐	....

1 Close
2 in your language!
3 down on the chair
4 Don't talk
5 up
6 Don't run
7 the bathroom door
8 Stand
9 Sit
10 your mother
11 Listen to
12 in school

Grammar: Giving instructions

2 Write the teacher's classroom rules.

CLASSROOM RULES

a ✔
b ✔
c Hello. How are you? ✔
d ✗
e ✗
f ✗

1 talk / English
   Talk in English. `c`
2 eat / classroom
   .... ☐
3 talk / friends
   .... ☐
4 listen / your teacher
   .... ☐
5 do / homework / evening
   .... ☐
6 run / classroom
   .... ☐

About you

3 Write three rules for your home. Choose from these words.

close	eat	listen	open	run

Don't run in the kitchen.
Don't eat in the living room.

1 ....
2 ....
3 ....

B Foundation exercises

Vocabulary: Activity verbs

1 Match the words/phrases with the pictures.

| dance | ~~play football~~ | play the guitar | ride a bike | sing | swim |

1 _play football_

2 ....

3 ....

4 ....

5 ....

6 ....

Grammar: can

2 Write the words in the correct order.

1 I   cook.   can't

I can't cook.

2 swim.   He   can

....

3 play football.   I   can't

....

4 can   act.   I

....

5 draw.   can't   She

....

6 can   speak English.   She

....

3 Complete the answers.

1 Can you sing?   Yes, _I can_ .

2 Can you make a cake?   No, ...

3 Can he swim?   Yes, ...

4 Can she draw?   No, ...

5 Can you dance?   Yes, ...

6 Can she play the guitar?   No, ...

B Activation exercises

Vocabulary: Activity verbs

1 Find six activity verbs. Write them below.

..........*sing*..........

K	U	E	V	S	I	N	G
L	D	R	A	W	R	E	T
E	A	J	O	I	E	C	K
N	N	P	B	M	A	O	S
A	C	T	Z	K	F	O	W
D	E	I	R	P	I	K	Q

....

....

....

....

....

2 Match the words to make activities. Then write.

1	ride
2	make
3	make
4	play
5	play
6	speak

| a cake |
| the guitar |
| Spanish |
| a birthday card |
| a bike |
| football |

1   *ride a bike*

2   ....

3   ....

4   ....

5   ....

6   ....

3 Find the activity verbs and write sentences.

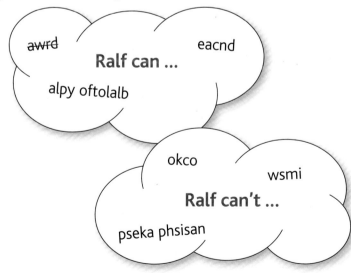

~~awrd~~   eacnd

Ralf can ...

alpy oftolalb

okco

wsmi

Ralf can't ...

pseka phsisan

1   *Ralf can draw.*   4   ....

2   5   ....

3   6   ....

Grammar: *can*

4 Find the correct stickers.

1

Lucy can't sing.

2

Peter can act.

3

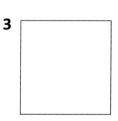

Kerrie can make a cake.

4

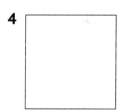

Freddy can't play the guitar.

5

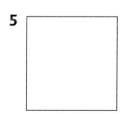

Ursula can't ride a bike.

6

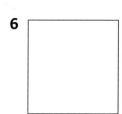

Tom can play football.

5 **2 53** Listen and answer *True* or *False*.

	True	False
1 Josh can dance.	✓	☐
2 He can sing.	☐	☐
3 He can't play the guitar.	☐	☐
4 Josh can cook.	☐	☐
5 Josh's mum can cook.	☐	☐
6 Josh's mum can't make cakes.	☐	☐

6 Look at Exercise 5. Write questions and answers about Josh and his mum.

1 *Can Josh dance?* ....
   Yes, he can. ....
2 ....
   ....
3 ....
   ....
4 ....
   ....
5 ....
   ....
6 ....
   ....

About you

7 Answer the questions about you.

1 Can you speak English? *Yes, I can.*
2 Can you draw? ....
3 Can you act? ....
4 Can you swim? ....
5 Can you ride a bike? ....
6 Can you play the guitar? ....

8 Complete the text with *can* or *can't*.

Meet Helen

This is Helen Dribblewell. Helen can do lots of things. She ¹(✓cook) *can cook* , and she ²(✓play) .... the guitar. She can act but she ³(✗ sing) .... and she can't dance! She ⁴(✓ride) .... a bike but she ⁵(✗ swim) .... But what's her favourite thing? Football! Yes, she ⁶(✓play) .... football, and she's really good.

Let's talk to Helen ...

9 Answer the questions about Helen.

1 Can Helen do lots of things? *Yes, she can.*
2 Can she cook? ....
3 Can she play the guitar? ....
4 Can Helen dance? ....
5 Can she swim? ....
6 Can she play football? ....

B Extension exercises

Vocabulary: Activity verbs

1 The words are mixed up! Find and write the verbs.

1 **acc**took .....*act*..... .....*cook*.....
2 **ma**dr**kaw**e ....
3 **ri**swi**d**e**m** ....
4 **spe**danak**ce** ....
5 **pala**cy**t** ....
6 **co**sino**kg** ....

2 Find and write the phrases.

1 ...*speak English*...
2 ....
3 ....
4 ....
5 ....
6 ....

Grammar: can

3 Write questions using the phrases from Exercise 2. Then write answers about you.

	Question	Your answer
1	*Can you speak English?*	*Yes, I can.*
2		
3		
4		
5		
6		

4 Write sentences with *and* and *but*.

		✓	✗
1	Raj	act, play football	speak Spanish
2	Miss Carr	dance, sing	act
3	Alex	sing, draw	swim
4	Mrs Patel	play the guitar, dance	ride a bike
5	Lily	act, dance	draw
6	Mrs Baker	draw, swim	make a cake

1 ...*Raj can act and play football but he can't* ...
   ...*speak Spanish.*...
2 ....
3 ....
4 ....
5 ....
6 ....

About you

5 Write sentences about your friends or family members.

My mum can speak Spanish but she can't speak English.

Friend/Family member 1

- ....
- ....
- ....

Friend/Family member 2

- ....
- ....
- ....

C Communication

Speaking: Make suggestions

1 Complete the dialogue.

Robbie: Look! There's a TV talent competition!

Alex: Wow! ¹ _Let's enter!_

Robbie: What can you do, Alex?

Alex: I can sing.

Lily: No, ² ...., Alex. But Robbie can sing and dance.

Robbie: I know, ³ .... a dance group.

Lily: ⁴ .... I can dance, too.

Alex: I can't dance. What can I do?

Lily: ⁵ .... draw a poster, and we can dance.

Alex: Cool! OK!

Lily: Let's practise!

Robbie: I can't now. ⁶ ....

Good idea!	let's start	I'm busy.
You can	~~Let's enter!~~	you can't

Your turn

2 Complete the dialogue.

At the TV talent competition.

Judge: Hello, what are your names?

Robbie: Robbie and Lily.

Judge: And ¹ _what can you do_ ?

Robbie: ² ....

Judge: ³ ....

Judge: Stop, stop!

Robbie: ⁴ ....

Judge: ⁵ .... Sorry!

Robbie: ⁶ .... go home, Lily.

Lily: ⁷ ....

Good idea.
We can sing and dance.
What's the matter?
Let's
~~what can you do~~
OK. Start.
You can't sing and you can't dance.

Writing: Start a club

3 Start a dance/singing group for a TV talent competition. Write a poster. Use the poster on page 63 of your Student's Book to help you.

Let's ....

I'm .... I .... but ....

Can ....? Can ....?

....

Come to ....

Send ....

Check

1 Choose the correct words to complete the text.

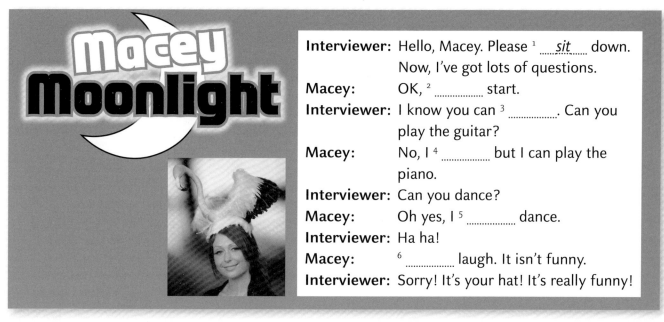

Macey Moonlight

Interviewer: Hello, Macey. Please ¹ ....*sit*.... down. Now, I've got lots of questions.

Macey: OK, ² .... start.

Interviewer: I know you can ³ .... Can you play the guitar?

Macey: No, I ⁴ .... but I can play the piano.

Interviewer: Can you dance?

Macey: Oh yes, I ⁵ .... dance.

Interviewer: Ha ha!

Macey: ⁶ .... laugh. It isn't funny.

Interviewer: Sorry! It's your hat! It's really funny!

1	A sit	B stand	C open	4	A can	B yes	C can't
2	A we	B don't	C let's	5	A can't	B cannot	C can
3	A ride	B sing	C make	6	A Not	B Don't	C Do

Score: ...... /5

2 Write the words and phrases in pairs.

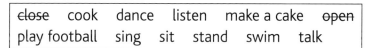

close   cook   dance   listen   make a cake   open
play football   sing   sit   stand   swim   talk

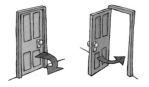

1 .....*open*..... .....*close*.....

2 ....

3 ....

4 ....

5 ....

6 ....

Score: ...... /5

Colour one ring on Lenny's tail for each correct answer.

My score is ....!

7 My routine

A Foundation exercises

Vocabulary: Sports

1 Look and complete the words.

1 s _w_ im _m_ i _n_ g   **2** te ___ n ___ s   **3** ho ___ k ___ y   **4** b ___ s ___ et ___ a ___ l

5 v ___ ll ___ y ___ all   **6** k ___ ra ___ e   **7** c ___ c ___ in ___   **8** at ___ l ___ ti ___ s

9 t ___ bl ___ te ___ n ___ s   **10** f ___ ot ___ a ___ l

Grammar: Present simple

2 Choose *do* or *don't*.

Do you like football?

Yes, I do.

1 A: Do you like football?   **B:** Yes, I *do* / *don't*.
2 A: Do you like cycling?   **B:** No, I *do* / *don't*.
3 A: Do you like tennis?   **B:** Yes, I *do* / *don't*.
4 A: Do you like hockey?   **B:** Yes, I *do* / *don't*.
5 A: Do you like karate?   **B:** No, I *do* / *don't*.
6 A: Do you like athletics?   **B:** No, I *do* / *don't*.

About you

3 Choose the correct answers for you.

1 A: Do you like swimming?
You: *Yes, I do. / No, I don't.*
2 A: Do you like cycling?
You: *Yes, I do. / No, I don't.*
3 A: Do you like basketball?
You: *Yes, I do. / No, I don't.*
4 A: Do you like volleyball?
You: *Yes, I do. / No, I don't.*
5 A: Do you like tennis?
You: *Yes, I do. / No, I don't.*
6 A: Do you like table tennis?
You: *Yes, I do. / No, I don't.*

Vocabulary: Sports

1 Look and write the sports.

| basketball | cycling | hockey | karate |
| table tennis | volleyball | | |

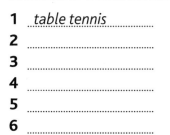

1 *table tennis*
2 ....
3 ....
4 ....
5 ....
6 ....

2 Find the words. Then complete the crossword.

1 ylicngc .... *cycling* ....
2 imgmswin ....
3 llbaetskba ....
4 csetthali ....
5 isnnte ....
6 bafollot ....

¹c
y
c
l
i
n
g

English today

3 Complete the dialogue.

| awesome | It's different. | they're boring | What's on |

Lottie: Hi Joe! ¹ .... *What's on* .... the TV?
Joe: A talent competition. Do you like talent competitions?
Lottie: No, ² ....
Joe: Let's see what's on the Sports Channel.
Lottie: Wow! It's basketball!
Joe: Do you like basketball?
Lottie: Yes, it's great. Look at Kobe Bryant. He's ³ ....!
Joe: I don't like basketball but I like cycling. ⁴ ....

Grammar: Present simple

4 Find the correct stickers.

1 I like cycling but I don't like athletics.

2 I don't like tennis but I like table tennis.

3 I like basketball but I don't like volleyball.

4 **A:** Do you like football?
  B: No, but I like hockey.

5 I like volleyball but I don't like swimming.

6 **A:** Do you like karate?
  B: Yes, I do.

5 Write sentences.

1 I / athletics   (✓) _I like athletics._
2 you / football   (✗) ....
3 I / hockey   (✗) ....
4 you / table tennis   (✓) ....
5 you / basketball   (✗) ....
6 I / karate   (✓) ....

6 Write questions from the sentences.

1 You like swimming. _Do you like swimming?_
2 You like basketball. ....
3 You like cycling. ....
4 You like football. ....
5 You like tennis. ....
6 You like karate. ....

About you

7 Write answers about you.

1 Do you like athletics? _Yes, I do./No, I don't._
2 Do you like swimming? ....
3 Do you like football? ....
4 Do you like karate? ....
5 Do you like cycling? ....
6 Do you like hockey? ....

8 Write sentences.

1 I ☺ football / I ☹ karate.
  I like football but I don't like karate.
2 I ☺ ice cream / I ☹ fish.
  ....
  ....
3 You ☺ monkeys / you ☹ snakes.
  ....
  ....
4 You ☺ cats / you ☹ dogs.
  ....
  ....
5 I ☺ basketball / I ☹ tennis.
  ....
  ....
6 You ☺ purple / you ☹ brown.
  ....
  ....

A Extension exercises

Vocabulary: Sports

1 Complete the sports words.

1 b _asketball_

2 s

3 c

4 h

5 k

6 t   t

Grammar: Present simple

2 Positive or negative? Read and tick (✓) the correct boxes.

	☺	☹
1 You like football.	✓	☐
2 You don't like volleyball.	☐	☐
3 You like penguins.	☐	☐
4 You don't like snakes.	☐	☐
5 You like bunk beds.	☐	☐
6 You don't like camping.	☐	☐

3 Use Exercise 2 to write two more sentences with *I like ... but I don't like ...*

1 *I like football but I don't like volleyball.*
2
3

4 Complete the email.

| are   Do you like   Do you like   don't like |
| like   'm   'm   's   've got |

Hello,
How ¹ _____are_____ you today? I ²_____
happy. My favourite sport is on the TV –
athletics. I really ³ _____ athletics.
⁴ _____ athletics?
We ⁵ _____ swimming at school this
Friday. I ⁶ _____ not happy – I
⁷ _____ swimming. It ⁸ _____ boring.
What about you? ⁹ _____ swimming?
Bye!
Tom

About you

5 Answer the questions about you.

1 What's your favourite sport? _____
2 Can you swim? _____
3 Do you like swimming? _____
4 Do you like football? _____
5 Can you ride a bike? _____
6 Have you got a bike? _____

B Foundation exercises

Vocabulary: Transport

1 Look and write the words.

> bike   bus   ~~car~~   motorbike   taxi   underground train

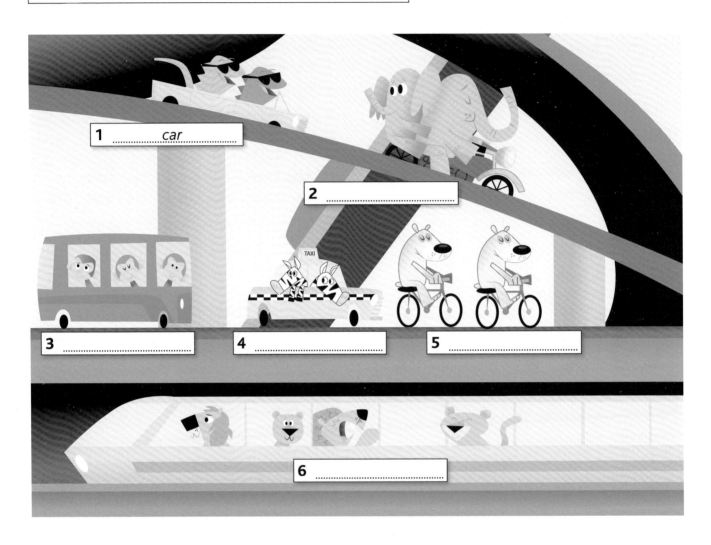

1 .... *car* ....

2 ....

3 ....

4 ....

5 ....

6 ....

Grammar: Present simple

2 Look at the picture in Exercise 1. Write the correct numbers.

1 (We go to school by bus.) `3`   4 (We go home by taxi.) ☐

2 (We go to school by car.) ☐   5 (We ride a motorbike to school.) ☐

3 (We ride our bikes home.) ☐   6 (We go home by underground train.) ☐

Vocabulary: Transport

1 **Match the words with the pictures.**

~~bike~~   boat   car   motorbike   plane   train

1   *bike*

2   ....

3   ....

4   ....

5   ....

6   ....

2 **Find and write the transport words.**

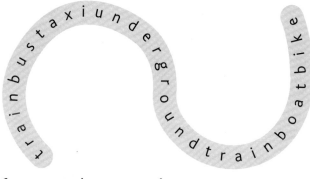

1   *train*   4   ....

2   5   ....

3   6   ....

Grammar: Present simple

3 **Write the words in the correct order.**

1   to   We   school.   walk

   We walk to school.

2   by   car.   go   home   We   don't

   ....

3   bikes   their   ride   They   to   school.

   ....

4   school   they   Do   go   to   by   car?

   ....

4 **You are Sam. Answer the questions.**

	Sam and Sunita (= we)	Kamal and Kate (= they)
1 ride bikes to school	✓	✗
2 go to football club	✓	✓
3 eat lunch at home	✗	✗
4 like TV	✓	✓
5 play basketball	✗	✗
6 play the guitar	✗	✓

1 A: Do you and Sunita ride bikes to school?

   You: *Yes, we do.*

2 A: Do Kamal and Kate go to football club?

   You: ....

3 A: Do Kamal and Kate eat lunch at home?

   You: ....

4 A: Do you and Sunita like TV?

   You: ....

5 A: Do you and Sunita play basketball?

   You: ....

6 A: Do Kamal and Kate play the guitar?

   You: ....

About you

5 **Answer the questions for you. Use _I_, _we_ and _they_.**

1 Do you talk to your friends at school? ....*Yes, I do.*.........
2 Do you and your friends go home by bus? ....
3 Do you walk home after school? ....
4 Do your friends ride bikes? ....
5 Do you and your friends go to a sports club? ....
6 Do your friends listen to music on an MP3 player? ....

6 **2 54** **Listen and number the pictures.**

a ....

b ....

c ....

d _1_

e ....

f ....

7 **Complete the email.**

| by bus | Do ... go | go | have | ~~like~~ | ride |

From: james354@123email.com
To: gemma723@123email.com
⌕ mynewbike.jpg

Hi Gemma!
Thank you for your email and photo. I ¹ ....*like*.... your dad's new car. My dad's got a new car, too. It's big and green. ² .... you .... to school by car? My brother and I ³ .... to school ⁴ .... But on Saturday mornings we ⁵ .... football club and we ⁶ .... our bikes to school.
I hope you like the photo of my new bike!
From,
James

8 **Write an email to James.**

To: james354@123email.com

Hi James!

Thank you for your ....

I go to school ....

.... On Saturday mornings

I ....

....

....

....

....

....

From,

....

Vocabulary: Transport

1 What are they?
Write the words.

1 ....*taxi*..............
2 ....
3 ....
4 ....
5 ....
6 ....

Grammar: Present simple

2 You are Lily Baker. Correct the sentences.

1 The Baker family live on Marble Road. (Market Road)
That's wrong. We *don't live on Marble Road. We live on Market Road.*

2 Robbie and Raj play football on Fridays. (basketball)
That's wrong. They ....
....

3 Lily, Asha and Vicky go to school by train. (walk)
That's wrong. We ....
....

4 Mr and Mrs Baker ride their bikes to work. (car)
That's wrong. They ....
....

3 Write Lily's questions.

1 (Asha and Raj) / go / school / bus?
Do they go to school by bus?

2 (Vicky and I) / walk / school?
....

3 (Alex and Robbie) / eat lunch / school?
....

4 (Asha and I) / ride our bikes / school?
....

5 (Mum and Dad) / go / work / car?
....

6 (My grandmother and grandfather) / go home / train?
....

About you

4 Write about you, where you live and how you go to school. Use these questions.

• Where do you live?
• How do you go to school?
• Do you go to school with your friends?
• What do you listen to on the bus?
• How do you go home from school?

I live ....
....
....
....

C Foundation exercises

Vocabulary: The time

 What time is it? Match the clocks with the times.

a	b	c
`07:00`	`06:45`	`03:30`

d	e	f
`09:00`	`10:30`	`02:15`

1 nine o'clock ......*d*....
2 half past three ....
3 seven o'clock ....
4 quarter to seven ....
5 half past ten ....
6 quarter past two ....

 **Complete the times. Use *past, half, to, quarter, o'clock*.**

1 ......*quarter*...... past nine

2 four ....

3 quarter .... nine

4 .... past five

5 .... past one

6 half .... seven

Grammar: Telling the time

 Complete the sentences.

~~half~~	It's	past	to	quarter	half

What time is it?

1 It's ......*half*...... past two.

2 It's quarter .... three.

3 .... six o'clock.

4 It's .... to twelve.

5 It's .... past nine.

6 It's quarter .... three.

 Choose the correct words.

1 They go to football practice *at*/ *in* one o'clock.

2 We ride our bikes *every* / *by* day.

3 They have basketball *at* / *on* Fridays.

4 They go home by car *on* / *at* four o'clock every day.

5 We eat lunch at home every *day* / *quarter*.

6 We go to bed at ten o'clock every *day* / *night*.

Vocabulary: The time

1 Write the times.

half   o'clock   past   quarter   to

1   *half past one*

2   ....

3   ....

4   ....

5   ....

6   ....

Grammar: Telling the time

2 What's wrong? Correct the times.

1 **3:30** It's half past two.
    No, it's half past three.

2 **6:30** It's quarter past six.
    ....

3 **11:45** It's quarter to eleven.
    ....

4 **8:30** It's half past nine.
    ....

5 **4:45** It's quarter past four.
    ....

6 **10:00** It's eleven o'clock.
    ....

3 Complete the sentences.

| at   at   every   every   On   ~~on~~ |

1 They go to basketball practice ....*on*....
    Mondays.

2 We have football practice .... week.

3 .... Thursdays we have computer club
    after school.

4 School starts .... half past eight.

5 I go to bed .... ten o'clock.

6 Do you ride your bike .... day?

4 Complete the text with *in*, *on* or *at*.

What's your favourite day?

I like Saturdays – we haven't got
lessons but I go to school [1] *on*
Saturday mornings. We have hockey
practice [2] .... ten o'clock. I go home
for lunch [3] .... half past twelve. [4] ....
the afternoon I have a guitar lesson.
My friends and I listen to music [5] ....
the evening and I go to bed [6] .... ten
o'clock.

5 Write the words in the correct order.

1 bike   day.   I   every   my   school   ride
    to
    I ride my bike to school every day.

2 basketball   We   Fridays.   play   on
    ....

3 at   lunch   They   don't   school.   eat
    ....

4 I   every   walk   to   morning.   school
    ....

5 home   car   go   in   They   by
    afternoon.   the
    ....

6 go   at   to   Saturdays.   bed   o'clock
    We   eleven   on
    ....

6 Write sentences about the sports programme.

SCHOOL SPORTS PROGRAMME

	MONDAY	TUESDAY	WEDNESDAY	THURSDAY	FRIDAY
Morning	9.45 Basketball	11.00 Swimming	10.00 Football	11.30 Tennis	
Afternoon	2.00 Table tennis	1.30 Athletics	2.45 Volleyball	1.15 Karate club	2.15 Cycling
After school	4.00 Football practice			4.30 Basketball practice	3.45 Swimming practice

1 Monday after school
(have) _They have football practice at four o'clock._

2 Thursday morning
(play) ....

3 Friday after school
(have) ....

4 Tuesday afternoon
(do) ....

5 Wednesday morning
(play) ....

6 Monday morning
(play) ....

About you

7 Write three more sentences about sports at your school.

1 _I have basketball practice on Fridays._

2 ....

3 ....
....

4 ....
....

English today

8 Complete the dialogues.

Remember?   See you later   Thanks for your watch is wrong   ~~Yum!~~

1 A: What's for lunch?

 B: Chips! _Yum!_

2 A: You've got football practice at four o'clock. ....

 B: Oh no, I'm late!

3 A: What time is it?

 B: It's half past one.

 C: No, it isn't. It's two o'clock –
....!

4 A: Hello, Aunt Lucy? ....
the birthday present. It's great!

 B: That's OK.

5 A: Hurry up, Joe. You're late for school!

 B: Oh no! ....,
Mum!

Vocabulary: The time

1 Draw the times on the clocks. Then write questions and answers.

7.45 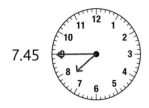   11.00 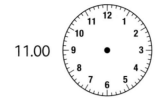   2.30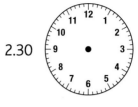

1 A: _What's the time?_
   B: _It's quarter to eight._

2 A: ....
   B: ....

3 A: ....
   B: ....

5.15 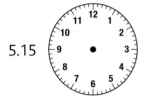   6.00 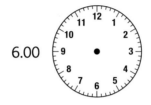   5.45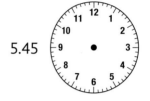

4 A: ....
   B: ....

5 A: ....
   B: ....

6 A: ....
   B: ....

Grammar: Telling the time

2 You are Sam. Write sentences about your week.

1 On Mondays
   I have a guitar lesson at quarter to four.

2 On Tuesdays
   ....

3 On Wednesdays
   ....

4 On Thursdays
   ....

5 On Fridays
   ....

6 On Saturdays
   ....

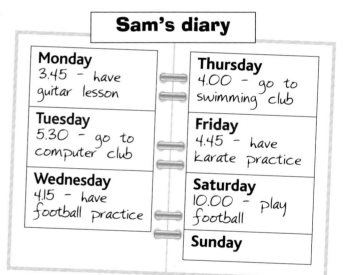

Sam's diary

Monday
3.45 – have guitar lesson

Tuesday
5.30 – go to computer club

Wednesday
4.15 – have football practice

Thursday
4.00 – go to swimming club

Friday
4.45 – have karate practice

Saturday
10.00 – play football

Sunday

3 Complete Jenny's blog with *on* or *at*.

Hi everyone!

I like Saturdays and Sundays! We don't have school. It's great! I have tennis practice ¹ _at_ ten o'clock ² ...... Saturdays and I have lunch ³ ...... one o'clock. I go to my friend Tricia's house ⁴ ...... three o'clock and we listen to music and play on the computer. ⁵ ...... Sundays my sister and I ride our bikes and ⁶ ...... two o'clock we eat lunch with Grandma and Grandad.

About you

4 Write your blog about Saturdays and Sundays. Use Exercise 3 to help you.

Hi everyone!

....
....
....
....
....

Check

1 **Choose the correct words to complete the text.**

My name's Jackie. I live on a farm in Australia with my mum, dad, two brothers and lots of animals! We ¹ ....*have*....... lessons at home – we haven't got a school here. Mum and Dad are our teachers! My brothers and I can speak Italian and we play the guitar. We do English ² .... day in the mornings and we play ³ .... and basketball ⁴ .... Tuesdays and Fridays. We ⁵ .... to school by bus. We walk ... to the living room! We have our lessons there. We ⁶ .... our home school!

1	**A** go	**B** have	**C** make	**4** **A** in	**B** on	**C** by
2	**A** after	**B** every	**C** by	**5** **A** don't like	**B** don't stop	**C** don't go
3	**A** football	**B** school	**C** taxi	**6** **A** start	**B** listen	**C** like

Score: .... /5

2 **Write the words in the correct columns.**

~~athletics~~ boat o'clock plane quarter volleyball

Sports	Transport	The time
...........*athletics*...........	....	....
....	....	....

Score: .... /5

Colour one ring on Lenny's tail for each correct answer.

My score is ....!

82

8 Work and play

A Foundation exercises

Vocabulary: Routines

1 Match the words with the pictures.

1 get dressed ...c...   **3** get up ......   **5** go to bed ......   **7** go to school ......
2 have breakfast ......   **4** have dinner ......   **6** have lunch ......   **8** wake up ......

Grammar: Present simple

2 Choose the correct words.

1 He *work / works* at night.
2 He *don't / doesn't* eat cornflakes.
3 He *have / has* lunch at two o'clock.

4 She *get / gets* up at seven o'clock.
5 She *go / goes* to school at nine o'clock.
6 She *doesn't / don't* play tennis.

3 Complete the answers about Mr Patel. Use *does* or *doesn't*.

1 A: Does he work at night?
   B: Yes, he *does* .

2 A: Does he come home at night?
   B: No, he ....

3 A: Does he go to bed at night?
   B: No, he ....

4 A: Does he eat cornflakes for breakfast?
   B: Yes, he ....

5 A: Does he sleep during the day?
   B: Yes, he ....

6 A: Does he eat cornflakes for dinner?
   B: No, he ....

4 Complete the table.

+	-	?
I work	I don't work	Do I work?
You ¹ *work*	You ⁴ .... work	⁹ .... you work?
We work	We don't ⁵	Do ¹⁰ .... work?
They ²	They ⁶	Do they ¹¹ .... ?
He works	He ⁷ .... work	Does he ¹² .... ?
She ³	She ⁸	¹³ .... she work?

A Activation exercises

Vocabulary: Routines

1 Match the words with the correct verbs.

| breakfast   to bed   dinner   dressed |
| to school   ~~up~~ |

GET	**1**	_up_
	2	
GO	**3**	
	4	
HAVE	**5**	
	6	

2 What do you do at these times? Write.

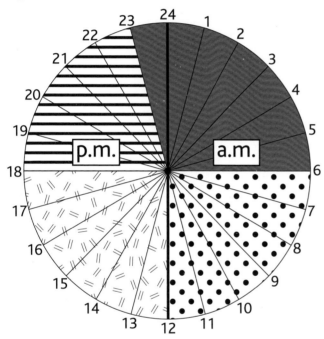

1 6.00 a.m. ➜ 12.00 p.m.
   wake up, get up

2 12.00 p.m. ➜ 6.00 p.m.

3 6.00 p.m. ➜ 11.00 p.m.

Grammar: Present simple

3 Choose the correct words.

1 She *work* / *works* during the day.

2 He *gets* / *get* up at four o'clock in the morning.

3 She *ride* / *rides* her bike to school every day.

4 He *go* / *goes* to bed at ten o'clock.

5 She *have* / *has* lunch at school at one o'clock.

6 He *wakes* / *wake* up late on Saturdays.

4 Find the correct stickers.

1 He gets up at eight o'clock.

2 He goes to school at half past eight in the morning.

3 She has lunch at one o'clock.

4 She gets dressed at quarter to eight.

5 He has dinner at seven o'clock in the evening.

6 She wakes up at quarter past six in the morning.

5 Correct the sentences.

1 Robbie's dad works at night. (during the day)

Robbie's dad doesn't work at night. He works during the day.

2 Robbie's friend rides his bike to school. (go by bus)

3 Lily eats crisps for lunch. (fruit)

4 Alex plays basketball in the afternoon. (football)

5 Mrs Baker makes cakes every day. (on Sundays)

6 Mr Patel sleeps at night. (during the day)

6 Write questions and answers about the people in Exercise 5.

1 he / work / night?   A: *Does he work at night?*   B: *No, he doesn't.*
2 he / ride / bike / school?   A: B:
3 she / eat / fruit / lunch?   A: B:
4 he / play / hockey / the afternoon?   A: B:
5 she / make cakes / Sundays?   A: B:
6 he / sleep / during the day?   A: B:

English today

7 Complete the dialogue.

funny   kidding

Alice: Sam, hurry up! We're late for tennis practice.

Sam: ¹ That's _____. Where are my glasses?

Alice: They're on your head, silly!

Sam: ² You're _____! Oh yes, they are!

8 Complete the text.

~~don't go~~   get up   go   have   have   have

I'm Anita Dorrick and I'm thirteen years old. I act in films so I ¹ *don't go* to school every day. What's my routine? I ² _____ at four o'clock in the morning! I start work at five o'clock. I ³ _____ lunch at quarter past twelve and ⁴ I _____ lessons with a teacher at home in the afternoon. In the evening ⁵ I _____ my dinner at seven o'clock and ⁶ I _____ to bed at eight o'clock.

9 Read the text in Exercise 8 and answer the questions.

1 Does she act in films?
Yes, she does.
2 Does she go to school every day?

3 What time does she get up?
She
4 When does she have lunch?
She
5 Where does she have lessons in the afternoon?
She
6 What time does she go to bed?
She

About you

10 Write four sentences about a daily routine in your notebook. Write about a friend or family member.

My friend's name is Anne. She gets up at seven o'clock. She ...

A Extension exercises

Vocabulary: Routines

1 Match the words to make phrases. Then write.

1 wake		**a** dinner		**1**	*wake up*	
2 have		**b** up		**2**		
3 get		**c** lunch		**3**		
4 have		**d** dressed		**4**		
5 go		**e** breakfast		**5**		
6 have		**f** to school		**6**		

2 Mrs Baker is talking to Robbie. Complete the sentences.

get dressed   get up   go to bed   go to school   have breakfast   ~~wake up~~

Morning

1 Come on, *wake up* ! It's seven o'clock. You've got school today!

2 Come on, ...! Don't sleep now.

3 Come on, ...! Here are your trousers and jumper.

4 Come on, ...! Here are your cornflakes!

5 Come on, ...! You're late for your lesson.

Evening

6 Come on, ...! It's ten o'clock. It's time to sleep now.

Grammar: Present simple

3 Look at Winston's Saturday routine. Write sentences about him.

1 *He gets up at seven o'clock in the morning.*

2 ....

3 ....

4 ....

5 ....

6 ....

Saturday	
7.00	get up
7.15	have breakfast
9.45	go to tennis club
10.30	play basketball
12.00	have lunch
Afternoon	talk to friends, listen to music

4 Write questions and answers about Winston.

1 get up / 8.00?
A: *Does he get up at eight o'clock?*
B: *No, he doesn't. He gets up at seven o'clock.*

2 have breakfast / 7.15?
A: ....
B: ....

3 go to tennis club / 7.45?
A: ....
B: ....

4 play football / 10.30?
A: ....
B: ....

5 have lunch / 12.00?
A: ....
B: ....

6 have dinner / afternoon?
A: ....
B: ....

About you

5 Write about your dad's or your mum's daily routine in your notebook.

My dad's name is Richard. He gets up at ...

Vocabulary: Snack food

1 **Look and write the snack foods.**

| banana | sandwich | bar of chocolate | ~~packet of crisps~~ | biscuits | burger | yoghurt | hot dog |

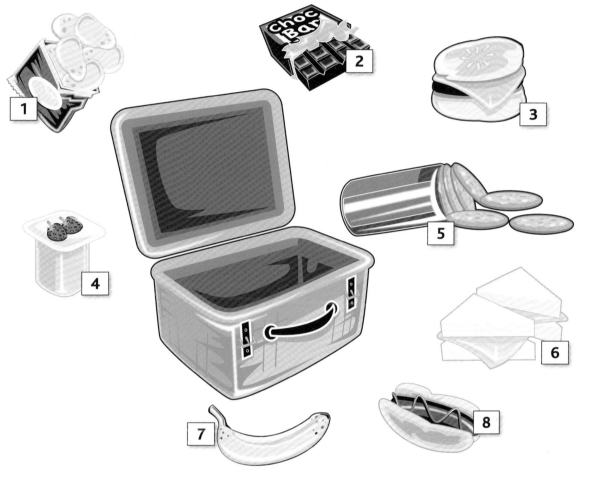

1 _packet of crisps_   3 ....   5 ....   7 ....

2 ....   4 ....   6 ....   8 ....

Grammar: Asking for permission

2 **Choose the correct words.**

1 A: (Can) / Can't I go home?

  B: No, you can / (can't).

2 A: Can / Can't we have a bar of chocolate?

  B: Yes, you can / can't.

3 A: Can / Can't I take a photo of you?

  B: No, you can / can't. Sorry.

3 **Complete the sentences with can or can't.**

1 A: ....._Can_..... I have an apple?

  B: Yes, you ...._can_.....

2 A: .... I watch a film?

  B: No, you ....

3 A: .... we be in your photo?

  B: Yes, you ....

4 A: .... we have a picnic here?

  B: No, you ....

B Activation exercises

Vocabulary: Snack food

1 Find and write the snack foods.

1 rgbeur   *burger*
2 ghtyour   ....
3 tho gdo   ....
4 ckpeat fo iscrsp   ....
5 rba fo ocatchole   ....
6 nabaan   ....

2 **2 55** **Listen and number the pictures.**

a ......
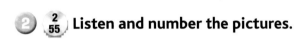

b ......

c _1_

d ......

e ......

f ......

Grammar: Asking for permission

3 Match the words to make questions.

1 Can I close   a Asha in the afternoon?
2 Can we eat   b the zoo on Saturday?
3 Can I see   c the door?
4 Can we watch   d on the computer?
5 Can we go to   e TV now?
6 Can I play   f lunch now?

4 Complete the sentences.

1 A: _____Can_____ I have a banana?
   B: Yes, you ....
2 A: .... I open the window?
   B: No, you ....
3 A: Can we have lunch now?
   B: Yes, ...
4 A: Can I open the door?
   B: No, ...
5 A: .... I eat a burger?
   B: No, you ....
6 A: Can I come to your house?
   B: Yes, ...

5 Write the questions for the situations.

1 You're cold.   (close / window)
   Can I close the window?
2 You're hungry.   (eat / banana)

3 You're tired.   (go to bed)

4 You're bored.   (play football)

5 You're hot.   (open / door)

6 You're sad.   (go to my room)

6 Write the words in the correct order.

1 A: we | Can | go | now? | home   _Can we go home now?_
   B: we | Yes, | can.   _Yes, we can._

2 A: in the evening? | Can | I | to your house | come   ....
   B: you | can. | Yes, ...

3 A: have | Can | we | for lunch? | sandwiches   ....
   B: we | No, | can't.   ....

4 A: I | to my friend's house | go | in the afternoon? | Can   ....
   B: can't! | you | No, ...

5 A: we | Can | go | on | Saturday? | to the zoo   ....
   B: Yes, | can. | we   ....

6 A: the | window? | open | Can | I   ....
   B: you | Yes, | can.   ....

7 Complete the questions in the dialogue.

Alex: Mum, ¹ .... _can I have breakfast_ .... (have breakfast) now?
Mrs Baker: Yes, you can. Here you are.
Alex: Thanks! ... Mum, ² .... (have a banana)?
Mrs Baker: OK, yes you can.
Alex: Mum, ³ .... (have a cake)?
Mrs Baker: Oh, OK. Yes you can.
Alex: Mum, ⁴ .... (eat a biscuit)?
Mrs Baker: A biscuit? Oh, OK. Yes, you can.
Alex: Mum, ⁵ .... (go to see Raj) later?
Mrs Baker: No, you can't!
Alex: Oh, Mum, ⁶ .... (go to bed)? I'm ill.
Mrs Baker: Alex, don't eat lots of cakes and biscuits!

English today

8 Match the phrases with the pictures. There is one extra picture.

| Move!   You're in the way! |

  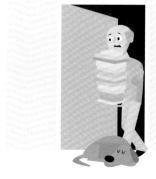

1 .... **2** .... **3** ....

B Extension exercises

Vocabulary: Snack food

1 The words are mixed up! Find and write the snack foods.

1. banwich
2. hot crisps
3. burcuit
4. packet of dog
5. sandhurt
6. yogana
7. bisger

1 _banana_
2 ....
3 ....
4 ....
5 ....
6 ....
7 ....

Grammar: Asking for permission

2 Write the questions.

1 | I | | can | go home.

Can I go home? ....

2 I can help you.

....

3 We can eat lunch now.

....

4 We can have a picnic.

....

5 I can have a packet of crisps.

....

6 I can watch TV.

....

3 Complete the dialogue. Use *can*.

Teacher: OK, [1] _____*can we start*_____ (we start)?

Student: [2] ....
(I sing and dance now)?

Teacher: You can sing but don't dance. Sit down and play the guitar.

Student: Oh, OK. ... Excuse me, [3] ....
.... (I talk to you)?

Teacher: Yes, sure.

Student: I'm hungry. [4] ....
.... (I have a sandwich)?

Teacher: No, you can't eat now.

Student: [5] ....
(I go home and eat)?

Teacher: No, you can't!

Student: I'm hot, too. [6] ....
.... (I open the window)?

About you

4 What do you ask your mum and dad? Write three questions and answers.

1 **A:** _Can I have a dog?_ ....
  B: _No, you can't._ ....

2 **A:** ....
  B: ....

3 **A:** ....
  B: ....

4 **A:** ....
  B: ....

Speaking: Buy food and drink

1 Complete the dialogue.

Mrs White: Hello, can I help you?

Bonnie: Yes, can I have a sandwich, please?

Mrs White: [1] *Yes, certainly. Anything else?* ....

Bonnie: [2] ....

Mrs White: The bananas are fifty pence each, and the apples are forty-five pence each.

Bonnie: [3] ....

Mrs White: Here you are.

Bonnie: [4] ....

Mrs White: [5] ....

Bonnie: Here's three pounds.

Mrs White: [6] ....
Bye!

Can I have a banana and an apple, please?

That's two pounds eighty.

Thank you. Here's your change.

Yes, how much are the bananas and the apples?

How much is that altogether?

~~Yes, certainly. Anything else?~~

Your turn

2 Complete the dialogue.

Mrs White: (can / help you)

Hello, [1] *can I help you* ....?

You: (can / have / sandwich)

Yes, [2] ....?

Mrs White: (yes / anything else)

[3] ....

You: (no / how much / that)

[4] ....

Mrs White: (£2.50)

[5] ....

You: (here / are)

[6] ....

Mrs White: Thanks. Have a nice day!

Writing: Design a menu

3 Read the dialogue and complete the menu.

COOL SNACKS MENU

Sandwiches (cheese/chicken)	[1]£ *2.80*
[2]	£3.20
Apples/Bananas	[3] ....p
Ice creams	£1.85
Cola	[4]£..........
Cakes	[5] ....p

Raj: Yum, chicken sandwiches. How much are they?

Man: They're two pounds eighty.

Lily: How much are the burgers?

Man: They're three pounds twenty.

Raj: Do you want an apple, too?

Lily: Oh yes! How much are they?

Man: The bananas and apples are forty-five pence each.

Raj: And how much is a cola?

Man: It's one pound ten. Anything else?

Raj: Yes, how much is a cake?

Man: Fifty pence.

Raj: Oh, OK.

Your turn

4 Write a menu for a snack shop. Use Exercise 3 to help you.

COOL SNACKS MENU

....	....
....	....
....	....
....	....
....	....

Check

1 **Read the text and answer the questions.**

Sue and the animals

This is Sue. She works at a zoo. She works with the parrots and the elephants. She gets up at five o'clock in the morning. The elephants eat their breakfast at six o'clock. What do they eat? They like apples and bananas but they don't like snack food. Let's talk to Sue.

A: Sue, can we talk to you?
Sue: Certainly.
A: What time do the elephants have lunch?
Sue: They have lunch at one o'clock.
A: Do you like your work?
Sue: Yes, I do.
A: What are your favourite animals?
Sue: The elephants and the parrots, of course!

1 Where does Sue work? *She works at a zoo.*
2 What animals does she work with? She ....
3 What time does she get up? She ....
4 Do the elephants like snack food? ....
5 When do the elephants have lunch? They ....
6 Does Sue like her work? ....

2 **Match the words to make phrases.**

Score: ...... /5

1 have   **a** to bed
2 get   **b** dressed
3 a packet   **c** of chocolate
4 wake   **d** dinner
5 a bar   **e** of crisps
6 go   **f** up

Score: ...... /5

Colour one ring on Lenny's tail for each correct answer.

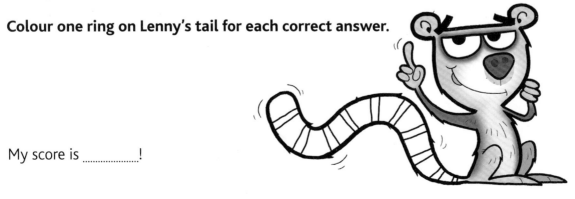

My score is ....!

Picture dictionary

1 Hello!

Family members

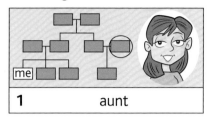

1 aunt

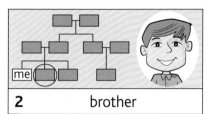

2 brother

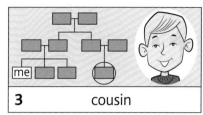

3 cousin

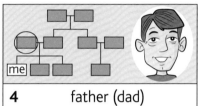

4 father (dad)

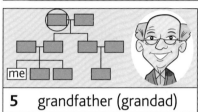

5 grandfather (grandad)

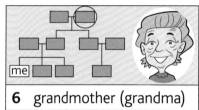

6 grandmother (grandma)

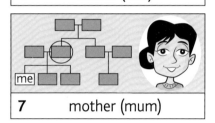

7 mother (mum)

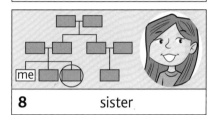

8 sister

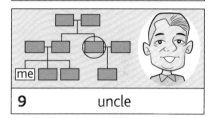

9 uncle

2 Favourite things

Possessions (1)

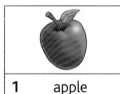

1 apple

2 bike

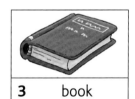

3 book

4 camera

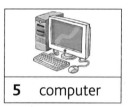

5 computer

6 football

7 ice cream

8 skateboard

9 TV

10 umbrella

Everyday objects

1 bag

2 comic

3 dictionary

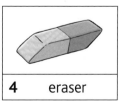

4 eraser

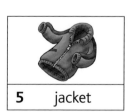

5 jacket

6 mobile phone

7 notebook

8 pen

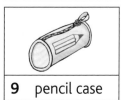

9 pencil case

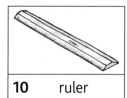

10 ruler

3 Wild world

Feelings

1 cold	2 happy	3 hot	4 hungry	5 ill	6 sad	7 thirsty	8 tired

Wild animals

1 crocodile	2 elephant	3 giraffe	4 lion	5 monkey
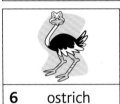				
6 ostrich	7 parrot	8 polar bear	9 snake	10 zebra

4 In my room

Clothes

1 dress	2 hat	3 jacket	4 jeans	5 jumper

6 shoes	7 skirt	8 trainers	9 trousers	10 T-shirt

Furniture

	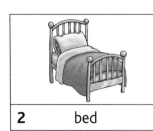	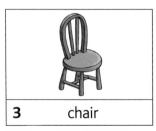	
1 bath	2 bed	3 chair	4 cooker
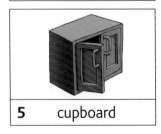		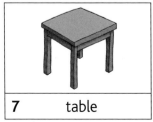	
5 cupboard	6 sofa	7 table	

5 People and pets

Possessions (2)

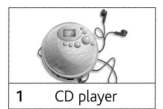

| 1 | CD player |

| 2 | MP3 player |

| 3 | pair of sunglasses |

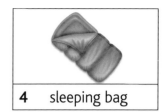

| 4 | sleeping bag |

| 5 | tent |

| 6 | torch |

| 7 | watch |

Pets

| 1 | bird |

| 2 | cat |

| 3 | dog |

| 4 | fish |

| 5 | hamster |

| 6 | lizard |

| 7 | rabbit |

| 8 | tortoise |

Parts of animals

| 1 body | 2 ear | 3 feet | 4 head | 5 leg | 6 nose | 7 paw | 8 tail | 9 wing |

6 Action!

Activity verbs

| 1 | act |

| 2 | cook |

| 3 | dance |

| 4 | draw |

| 5 | make (a cake) |

| 6 | play (football) |

| 7 | play (the guitar) |

| 8 | ride (a bike) |

| 9 | sing |

| 10 | speak (Spanish) |

| 11 | swim |

7 My routine

Sports

1 athletics

2 basketball

3 cycling

4 football

5 hockey

6 karate

7 swimming

8 table tennis

9 tennis

10 volleyball

Transport

1 bike

2 boat

3 bus

4 car

5 motorbike

6 plane

7 taxi

8 train

9 underground train

8 Work and play

Routines

1 get dressed

2 get up

3 go to bed

4 go to school

5 have breakfast

6 have dinner

7 have lunch

8 wake up

Snack food

1 banana

2 bar of chocolate

3 biscuits

4 burger

5 hot dog

6 packet of crisps

7 sandwich

8 yoghurt

Stickers

Unit 1B, Activation, Exercise 2

 Paolo

 Perlita

 Enzo

 Belinda

 Elena

 Alberto

Unit 2A, Activation, Exercise 4

Unit 3C, Activation, Exercise 1

Unit 4A, Activation, Exercise 4

Unit 5B, Activation, Exercise 5

Unit 6B, Activation, Exercise 4

Unit 7A, Activation, Exercise 4

Unit 8A, Activation, Exercise 4